THE COMPLETE BOOK
OF FOOTBALL TRIVIA

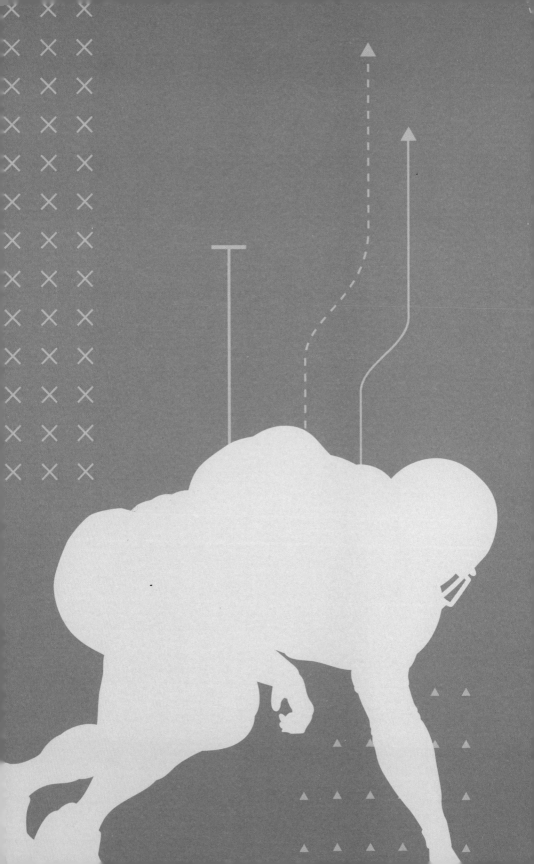

THE COMPLETE BOOK OF

FOOTBALL TRIVIA

TEST YOUR KNOWLEDGE WITH

750
QUESTIONS

JERRETT HOLLOWAY

callisto publishing
an imprint of Sourcebooks

I would like to dedicate this book to my two older brothers, James and Jamaal. Thanks for always setting a great example and consistently raising the bar for me to chase after.

Copyright © 2024 by Callisto Publishing LLC
Cover and internal design © 2024 by Callisto Publishing LLC
Images by Alamy: © Al Golub/ZUMA Wire: cover top left; © Russell Tracy/Southc/
ZUMA Press: cover top right; © Scott A. Miller/ZUMA Wire: cover bottom right
Creative Market: © GOAT Design Co (diagrams); © Christos Georghiou
and © charnsitr (player silhouettes)
Art Director: Lisa Schreiber
Art Producer: Stacey Stambaugh
Editor: Adrian Potts
Production Editor: Rachel Taenzler
Production Manager: Martin Worthington

Callisto and the colophon are registered trademarks of Callisto Publishing LLC

Published by Callisto Publishing LLC C/O Sourcebooks LLC
P.O. Box 4410, Naperville, Illinois 60567-4410
(630) 961-3900
callistopublishing.com

Library of Congress Cataloging-in-Publication Data is on file with the publisher.

Printed and bound in China.
OGP 10 9 8 7 6 5 4 3 2 1

CONTENTS

INTRODUCTION

Welcome to *The Complete Book of Football Trivia*!

As a lifelong fan of the National Football League, I know that part of what brings people together on game day—and every day, when speaking about football—is trivia. That's because trivia sparks conversation, and who doesn't love a lively conversation about football? This book will allow you to test your own knowledge of the NFL, its rich history, and the more recent highlights that have helped make the game what it is and etch its place in American society.

What makes the NFL fun for most fans is how every season takes on a life of its own. Some unexpected teams can surprise us with how they play, while others don't meet expectations and go from contender to pretender. Games can change on a single play or penalty, seasons can change on one game, and the future of every franchise can rise and fall with each win or loss. So much of this ebb and flow is because the game of football changes from year to year. From the Wildcat to the Run-Pass Option, defenses spend the off-season trying to stop what they saw last year, while offenses try to add a new wrinkle that will make it easier to score when they need it most.

This trivia book will offer every reader a chance to learn or remember how much the NFL has changed over the decades by looking at the greatest players, teams, and games. You will be quizzed on the league's all-time greats and the dynasty teams that made their mark from decade to decade, as well as the coaches, franchise owners, and others who helped them succeed. These questions will inspire conversation and debate while also challenging everyone to remember facts and details.

This trivia book was born out of the passion I have for the NFL, and I want to bring that passion out in you by challenging your knowledge of all things NFL. I also hope this trivia book brings everyone who reads it hours of entertainment, while also connecting you to fellow fans or, even better, bringing a new fan to the game.

HOW TO USE THIS BOOK

The Complete Book of Football Trivia **has been laid out in a very** easy-to-use format, with all of the questions grouped by category for easy navigation. In chapter 1, questions about all thirty-two teams are arranged by conference and division, making it easier for you to find a question to surprise a rival fan or test your own knowledge of your favorite team. I promise fans of every team in the league will see trivia questions written specifically for them. That doesn't mean that general NFL fans won't be able to answer these questions. But every team is important to the league, so they each will get a highlight.

Starting with chapter 2 and going forward, the questions are, in general, categories covering players and coaches, bloopers and memorable games, as well as the biggest game of every season: the Super Bowl. This book also tests your knowledge of the Hall of Fame—those legendary players, coaches, and team executives who helped shape NFL dynasties. This book is boredom-proof since there are seven chapters of questions, each providing its own set of challenges to the reader and those they are sharing the trivia questions with. And when you and your friends are finally stumped, you can find the answers to all the questions in the back of the book.

So sit back, relax, grab a paper and a pen to keep score, and see how many questions you can get right without help from your phone. In the process, find out how much you really know about the history of the NFL and your own team, as well as those who made history and shaped the game into what it is today—on the field, on the sidelines, and in the front office. Along the way, I hope you have some laughs and find out something you did not know before picking up *The Complete Book of Football Trivia*!

CHAPTER 1

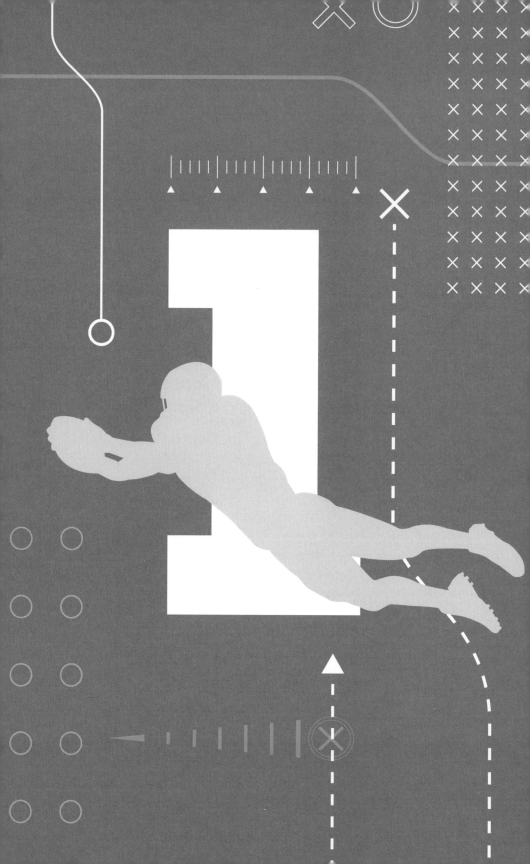

THE DRAFT

As teams prepare to battle for wins during the NFL regular season, their scouts are also preparing. Except the scouts prepare for the NFL Draft, which is the centerpiece of football's off-season. Much like the Super Bowl, commentators prepare for the draft months in advance as they look to find out anything and everything they can about every player who could hear their name called. Likewise, fans have taken to enjoying all three days of the NFL Draft by either attending it or having parties, as their favorite teams hopefully draft their next great players.

If you don't have time to watch college football games from every state university, or even half the schools with Bulldogs or Wildcats as mascots, try and catch one of the many NFL media Mock Drafts that take place in anticipation of the actual draft. While these Mock Drafts are normally based on false information provided to the media, they do offer some insight into players' best and worst traits. They are also one of the rare times when those in the media have work that can be graded, with even the best Mock Drafts only having a handful of first-round picks.

GENERAL

1. Who are the only two Heisman Trophy winners who were not selected in the NFL Draft since 1967?

2. In 2021, Peyton Manning became the fourth quarterback drafted first overall to be inducted into the Pro Football Hall of Fame. Who were the first three quarterbacks to achieve this honor?

3. Who was the last player drafted by two different NFL teams?

4. Who was the last running back taken first overall in an NFL Draft?
   a. Eddie George
   b. Lawrence Phillips
   c. Marshall Faulk
   d. Ki-Jana Carter

5. Name the AFL's only first overall draft pick to make the Pro Football Hall of Fame.

6. Name the three running backs selected first overall to win NFL Rookie of the Year honors.

7. Name the three quarterbacks selected first overall to win NFL Rookie of the Year honors.

8. Name the three franchises who have never selected first overall in any NFL Draft.

9. _____ is the last quarterback selected by the New Orleans Saints in the first round of the NFL Draft.

10. In 2019, which three colleges became locked in a tie for the record of having five players each selected first overall in the NFL Draft?

11. As of 2023, what are the last two franchises to draft Heisman Trophy winners in back-to-back seasons?

12. Which quarterback drafted in 1983 became an NFL head coach in 2019?

13. Who was the last wide receiver taken first overall in an NFL Draft?

    a. Calvin Johnson

    b. Marvin Harrison

    c. Keyshawn Johnson

    d. Larry Fitzgerald

14. Who is the last placekicker drafted in the first round of an NFL Draft?

15. Can you name the five Hall of Fame players selected in the 1985 NFL Draft?

16. Guard Russ Grimm is the only offensive player from the 1982 Draft to have reached the Hall of Fame, along with six defensive players from the same draft class. Can you name them?

17. _____ is the only Heisman Trophy winner to also become an NFL head coach.

18. Who are the only two first overall picks between 2000 and 2010 to win at least one Super Bowl?

19. Who is the only first overall draft pick from 2010 to 2019 to be on a Super Bowl–winning team?

20. Which two quarterbacks were selected ahead of future Hall of Famer Brett Favre in the 1991 Draft?

21. Which college conference had the most players (65) drafted during the 2022 NFL Draft?

22. After team records, what is the next tiebreaker the NFL uses to determine draft order?

23. What year was the NFL Draft first broadcast on television?

 **AFC East**

24. Which two future Hall of Famers were selected by the Buffalo Bills with the first overall pick?

25. True or False: The Miami Dolphins have not drafted any players who have made the Hall of Fame since Dan Marino in 1983.

26. Order these New England Patriots players by the draft pick the team used to select them: Tom Brady, Troy Brown, Julian Edelman, Rob Gronkowski, Adam Vinatieri.

27. Name the eight quarterbacks drafted by the New York Jets between 2010 and 2021.

28. Which 2021 NFL head coach was drafted by the New England Patriots in 2003?

29. The Miami Dolphins have had the first overall pick in the draft only one time. Who did they select?

30. True or False: The last player drafted by the New York Jets to make the Hall of Fame was Joe Namath.

31. Who was the first quarterback drafted by the Buffalo Bills after they took Jim Kelly in 1983?

32. Which two 1995 New England Patriots draft picks made the Pro Football Hall of Fame?

33. In 2018, Josh Allen became the _____ player taken by the Buffalo Bills from the University of Wyoming.

 **AFC North**

34. In the franchise's first quarter century of existence (1996 to 2021), the Baltimore Ravens drafted _____ players who reached the Hall of Fame.

35. What was the name of the first draft pick ever made by the Pittsburgh Steelers?

36. This quarterback drafted in 1971 entered the 2023 season as the Cincinnati Bengals, all-time yardage passing leader.

    a. Boomer Esiason

    b. Carson Palmer

    c. Andy Dalton

    d. Ken Anderson

37. True or False: The Cleveland Browns have not drafted a future Hall of Famer since 1980.

38. Who was the last quarterback drafted by the Cleveland Browns before their three-year hiatus, which lasted from 1996 to 1998 after owner Art Modell tried to move the team to Baltimore?

39. Which two college teammates were both drafted by the Cincinnati Bengals in 2001?

40. Put these players in order by the year they were drafted by the Pittsburgh Steelers:

    a. Mel Blount

    b. Terry Bradshaw

    c. Joe Greene

    d. Jack Ham

    e. Franco Harris

41. Name the two players drafted out of the University of Delaware to win a Super Bowl with the Baltimore Ravens.

42. From 2000 to 2020, name all the players drafted by the Pittsburgh Steelers who attended Michigan State.

43. Which wide receiver, drafted in 1998, has the most receptions of any wideout selected that year?

 **AFC South**

44. In the 1990s, the Indianapolis Colts drafted four future Hall of Famers in the first round. Name them.

45. In their first 20 Drafts, the Houston Texans selected two players from the University of Wisconsin. Name them.

46. _____ was the first player from Clemson University ever drafted by the Jacksonville Jaguars.

47. This 1996 first-round draft pick of the Houston Oilers became the franchise's all-time leading rusher after the franchise relocated and became the Tennessee Titans.

48. In their first 10 seasons in Tennessee (1997 to 2006), the Titans only used first-round draft picks on offensive players twice. Who were those two players?

49. Which two Hall of Fame quarterbacks were first overall draft picks by the Colts franchise?

50. Who was the first quarterback ever drafted by the Jacksonville Jaguars?

51. Twice in the 1990s, the Indianapolis Colts had two first-round draft picks, and each time they took a linebacker with their second pick. Name the two players chosen.

52. Name the only four University of South Carolina defensive players drafted by the Houston Texans.

53. Name the only placekicker ever drafted by the Houston Texans.

 **AFC West**

54. The Raiders were the first franchise to draft three left-handed quarterbacks. Can you name them?

55. Prior to Patrick Mahomes in 2017, who was the last quarterback the Kansas City Chiefs drafted in the first round?

56. What running back, drafted in the third round by the Denver Broncos in 2005, never played a game in the NFL?

57. Who were the first- and second-round draft picks of the San Diego Chargers in 2001?

58. True or False: Among wide receivers drafted in 2016, no player had more receptions or receiving yards than Kansas City's Tyreek Hill did in his first four seasons.

59. What future Hall of Famer was the Oakland Raiders' first-round draft pick in 1973?

60. This Denver Broncos draft pick from 1995 is one of two running backs from that class to make the Hall of Fame. Who is it?

61. Who's the first offensive player drafted by the San Diego Chargers to reach the Hall of Fame?

62. Name all four of the University of Southern California players who were drafted by the Oakland Raiders in the first round.

63. Since the 2000 Draft, the Kansas City Chiefs have drafted four wide receivers in the first round. Who were they?

64. Philadelphia Eagles' Hall of Fame safety Brian Dawkins was drafted in which round during the 1996 NFL Draft?

65. Philadelphia Eagles' Hall of Famer Reggie White was drafted in the first round of the 1984 NFL Supplemental Draft. Which pick was used to select him?

    a. First

    b. Fourth

    c. Fifth

    d. Tenth

66. True or False: The Philadelphia Eagles' six-time Pro Bowl quarterback Donovan McNabb was drafted first overall in the 1999 NFL Draft.

67. Which Hall of Fame New York Giants player was drafted second overall in the 1981 NFL Draft?

68. True or False: Hall of Fame defensive end Michael Strahan was drafted by the New York Giants in the second round of the 1993 NFL Draft.

69. The Washington Commanders all-time receiving leader Art Monk was drafted in which round during the 1980 NFL Draft?

    a. Sixth round

    b. Third round

    c. First round

    d. Second round

70. Which Hall of Fame Washington Commanders defensive back was drafted in the first round of the 1983 NFL Draft?

71. Which quarterback is the only one ever drafted by the Dallas Cowboys with the first overall pick?

    a. Roger Staubach

    b. Troy Aikman

    c. Tony Romo

    d. Vinny Testaverde

72. Which Super Bowl–winning wide receiver was drafted in the first round of the 1988 NFL Draft by the Dallas Cowboys?

73. _____ was the Dallas Cowboys' Super Bowl–winning running back who was drafted second overall in 1977.

74. In 1974, who became the first player from a historically Black college to be selected as the number-one pick in the NFL draft?

 **NFC North**

75. True or False: Hall of Fame running back Walter Payton was drafted first overall by the Chicago Bears in the 1975 NFL Draft.

76. Which linebacker was drafted by the Chicago Bears in the first round of the 2000 Draft?

    a. Brian Urlacher

    b. Lance Briggs

    c. Mike Singletary

    d. Khalil Mack

77. Which Pro Bowl wide receiver did the Green Bay Packers draft in the seventh round of the 1999 NFL Draft?

78. Which pick was used by the Green Bay Packers to draft quarterback Aaron Rodgers in the 2005 NFL Draft?

    a. First overall

    b. Tenth overall

    c. Eighteenth overall

    d. Twenty-fourth overall

79. Name the last Pro Bowl wide receiver that was drafted by the Green Bay Packers in the first round?

80. Who was the first-round wide receiver taken by the Detroit Lions in 2007?

81. Running back Barry Sanders is the Detroit Lions' all-time rushing leader. Which pick was used to select him in the 1989 NFL Draft?

    a. First overall

    b. Second overall

    c. Third overall

    d. Fifth overall

82. True or False: Five-time Pro Bowler Ndamukong Suh was drafted first overall by the Detroit Lions in the 2010 NFL Draft.

83. Name the two Minnesota Vikings wide receivers who were drafted in the first round since 1980 and also won Offensive Rookie of the Year.

84. Which pick did the Minnesota Vikings use to select Adrian Peterson in the 2007 NFL Draft?

    a. First overall

    b. Third overall

    c. Fifth overall

    d. Seventh overall

 **NFC South**

85. This first-round pick by the New Orleans Saints in the 2001 Draft became the franchise's all-time leading rusher.

86. True or False: The New Orleans Saints did not draft any wide receivers or tight ends in the first round between 2015 and 2021.

87. Which Heisman Trophy winner was drafted by the New Orleans Saints with the fifth overall pick in the 1999 NFL Draft?

88. In back-to-back drafts, the Carolina Panthers chose the Offensive Rookie of the Year and the Defensive Rookie of the Year. Name the players and the drafts.

89. True or False: The Carolina Panthers' all-time leading receiver, Steve Smith Sr., was drafted in the first round.

90. Who did the Atlanta Falcons select with the first overall pick in the 2001 NFL Draft?

91. Who were the two wide receivers the Atlanta Falcons drafted in the first round in back-to-back drafts?

92. The Tampa Bay Buccaneers drafted two future Hall of Famers in the first round of the same NFL Draft. Who were the players and which draft was it?

93. Which running back was drafted first overall by the Tampa Bay Buccaneers in the 1986 NFL Draft, yet never played for the team?

94. As part of the trade to acquire Jon Gruden, which two first-round picks were traded to the Oakland Raiders?

 **NFC West**

95. What round of the 2011 NFL Draft did the Seattle Seahawks take cornerback Richard Sherman?

    a. First round

    b. Third round

    c. Fifth round

    d. Sixth round

96. What two draft picks were used by the Seattle Seahawks to trade for quarterback Matt Hasselbeck?

97. True or False: The Seattle Seahawks' all-time passing leader, Russell Wilson, was drafted in the third round of the 2012 NFL Draft.

98. Name the most recent Hall of Fame running back that was drafted by the Los Angeles Rams in the first round.

99. Which quarterbacks were selected with the first overall pick by the St. Louis Rams and the Los Angeles Rams in 2010 and 2016, respectively?

100. What pick did the Arizona Cardinals use to draft Larry Fitzgerald in the 2004 NFL Draft?

    a. Third overall

    b. Fifth overall

    c. Seventh overall

    d. Tenth overall

101. True or False: Since 1980, the Arizona Cardinals have had the first overall pick in the NFL Draft only once.

102. Who was the 2010 Hall of Fame inductee that was drafted by the San Francisco 49ers in the first round?

103. In which round did the San Francisco 49ers select Joe Montana in the 1979 NFL Draft?

   a. First round

   b. Third round

   c. Fourth round

   d. Sixth round

104. True or False: Hall of Fame safety Ronnie Lott was drafted by the San Francisco 49ers in the top five of the 1981 NFL Draft.

105. Who was the quarterback drafted as "Mr. Irrelevant" that led the San Francisco 49ers to the NFC Championship Game in 2023?

106. Which fifth-round draft pick of the Los Angeles Rams broke a 63-year record for the most receiving yards for a rookie?

107. Which Seattle Seahawks cornerback, who was the fifth pick of the 2023 NFL Draft, ended his rookie season with 79 tackles, 12 pass breakups, and three sacks?

≡ NFL DRAFT TIMELINE ≡

From booing the commissioner to holding your breath to see what Mel Kiper Jr. thinks of your team's latest pick, every football fan undoubtedly recalls many memorable moments from the NFL Draft. Yet those who were at the first draft would be amazed at what it has turned into over the years.

The first draft was held in Philadelphia on February 6, 1936. Interestingly, one of the draft's guests of honor never attended the event or even played an NFL game. That's because first overall pick, Jay Berwanger, who had won the Heisman Trophy with the University of Chicago, chose to become a foam rubber salesperson as it sounded like a more stable career than being a football player.

Securing talented players was how the upstart AFL was able to force a merger with the NFL in the 1960s. One of the people who made that possible was AFL commissioner Al Davis. The Raiders

owner would attend college bowl games and bring contracts for drafted players to sign. One of those players, Lance Alworth from the University of Arkansas, signed his contract under the goalpost seconds after the 1962 Sugar Bowl ended.

It took until 1980 for ESPN to bring the NFL Draft to the fans by broadcasting it on television. Despite doubts from commissioner Pete Rozelle that anyone would watch, the new all-sports channel aired the NFL's National Selection Meeting, as it was officially called. Nowadays, the three-day event is attended by football fans in the host city and watched by millions on ESPN, as well as the NFL Network, with each providing instant analysis on the quality of every selection.

The NFL Draft has truly become an industry unto itself. In 2018, it brought in $125 million to its host city of Dallas, Texas. By 2019, the host-city haul had skyrocketed to $224 million, which is what Nashville, Tennessee, is said to have made for hosting the draft that year.

CHAPTER 2

TEAMS

Which NFL team are you a fan of? Did "America's Team," the Dallas Cowboys, catch your eye growing up? Or did you cheer the "Steel Curtain" defenses of the of Pittsburgh Steelers to victory? Was it the duo of head coach Bill Belichick and quarterback Tom Brady, who turned "the Pats" into a dynasty, that made you a fan? Or did you become infatuated by the success and intimidation of the Silver and Black Raiders?

The great thing about the NFL is that people build bonds with certain teams that last forever. Your favorite team is passed down to become your kids' favorite team and then your kids' kids' favorite team. The sense of community that is developed across a team's fan base extends the bond to not just the team, but also the city itself. The beauty of it all is that even when players change teams or teams relocate, you continue to root for your team because you can't forget the memories that team has given you, good or bad.

NAME THAT TEAM

108. What was the only NFL team to allow over 500 points in a 14-game season?

109. What are the only two teams to average less than 10 points scored per game for an entire season?

110. Which team holds the single-season record for the most penalties accepted and the most penalty yards marked against them?

111. Which franchise holds the record for the most consecutive seasons played without a playoff berth?

112. Which NFL franchise has gone the longest without winning an NFL championship or Super Bowl?

113. The 2020 New England Patriots had a losing record for the first time since 2000, ending a 19-year streak. Which franchise's record would they have tied with a 20th winning year?

114. From 1970 to 2020, which was the only franchise to win more than 60 percent of their games?

115. Between 1970 and 2020, 14 franchises won at least half their games. Of those teams, which is the only one that has never won a Super Bowl?

116. At 12 seconds, which franchise holds the record for the fastest points scored in a Super Bowl?

117. Which team scored the fastest touchdown in Super Bowl history, needing just 14 seconds to get in the end zone?

118. Which franchise holds the record for the fewest points allowed in a 14-game season?

119. Which franchise holds the record for the fewest points allowed in a 16-game season?

120. Which team has retired 14 jersey numbers, the most in the NFL history?

121. Name the six NFL franchises that have yet to retire a player's jersey number.

122. Which franchise is the only one remaining to have never reached a conference championship game?

123. Which franchise was the first to reach 3,000 rushing yards in a season?

124. Which NFL franchise has had two perfect regular seasons?

125. Name the only NFL franchise to win back-to-back-to-back championships.

126. Which franchise was the first to appear in three straight Super Bowls?

127. This NFL team entered the 2021 season having scored the most points in a single season.

128. Which franchise has won all of their Super Bowls over teams with an animal in their nickname?

129. Entering 2021, which franchise held the record for the most Super Bowl losses?

130. Which franchise's all-time leading passer(s) has the last name Carr:

   a. Raiders

   b. Texans

   c. Both the Raiders and the Texans

   d. Neither the Raiders nor the Texans

131. Which running back is the all-time leading rusher for the New England Patriots?

132. Which franchise entered the 2021 season with the best winning percentage in NFL history?

133. Which current NFL franchises are the only three with at least 700 victories in their history?

134. Between 1970 and 2020, which NFL franchise lost more than 60 percent of their games?

135. Between 2000 and 2020, which franchise only had one Hall of Famer wear their uniform—and only for one season?

136. Which are the five AFL franchises that have won Super Bowls?

137. Which franchise uses the same team colors as the other major professional sports teams in their home city?

138. Despite their distance from Hawai'i, which franchise chose "Honolulu Blue" as one of their colors?

139. Which franchise has been the only one to make four first-round picks in the same draft?

140. Which two rival teams have made trades involving head coaches two separate times?

141. After the 2021 NFL Hall of Fame induction ceremony, which three NFL franchises had their leading passer, rusher, receiver, and winningest head coach all in the Hall of Fame?

142. Which are the four teams that have appeared in and never lost a Super Bowl between 1967 and 2021?

143. What did the Washington Football Team change their official name to in 2022?

144. Which team finished the 2023 season with its 20th straight non-losing season?

145. In 2023, which team beat the New England Patriots' record for most postseason wins with their 38th playoff victory?

GAMES WITH NICKNAMES

146. Which two NFL teams played in the 1958 NFL Championship Game, widely known as "The Greatest Game Ever Played"?

    a. New York Giants and Chicago Bears

    b. Green Bay Packers and Baltimore Colts

    c. Baltimore Colts and New York Giants

    d. Chicago Bears and Green Bay Packers

147. Which two NFL teams played in the 1967 NFL Championship Game known as the "Ice Bowl"?

148. Which two NFL teams played in the 1999 AFC Wild Card game known as the "Music City Miracle," where the winning team scored a game-winning touchdown with only 16 seconds on the clock?

149. The _____ was a 1988 divisional playoff game that became legendary due to adverse conditions where players couldn't see what was happening.

150. Which two NFC East teams were involved in the 1989 Thanksgiving game known as the "Bounty Bowl," a game in which a $200 bounty was placed on the kicker?

    a. Dallas Cowboys and Washington Commanders

    b. Philadelphia Eagles and New York Giants

    c. Washington Commanders and New York Giants

    d. Dallas Cowboys and Philadelphia Eagles

151. Which two NFC East teams played in the "Miracle at the New Meadowlands," a game in which a recovered fumble turned into a touchdown to secure the win?

152. Which two teams played in the 1992 Wild Card game that is now known as "The Comeback," a game in which one team recovered from a 32-point deficit to win?

153. Which two teams played in the 1981 AFC Championship Game known as "The Freezer Bowl," a game played in -9° F with wind chills between -30° F and -50° F?

154. Which two teams played in the 1986 AFC Championship Game that has now become known as "The Drive," which had a legendary offensive series in the fourth quarter that tied the game?

155. Which two teams played in the 1987 AFC Championship Game that has now become known as "The Fumble," a game in which a player fumbled at the one-yard line and sealed his team's fate?

MASCOTS AND LOGOS

156. What is the name of the old New England Patriots logo, which was used from the 1960s until 1993?

157. When was the current Philadelphia Eagles logo first adopted?

    a. 1990

    b. 1993

    c. 1996

    d. 2000

158. What does the Dallas Cowboys logo represent?

159. True or False: 49ers mascot Sourdough Sam is a gold miner.

160. After what famous poet is the Baltimore Ravens mascot named?

161. Billy the Buffalo became the official Buffalo Bills mascot in what year?

162. In what year did the dolphin in the Miami Dolphins logo start going without a helmet?

163. Steely _____ is the name of the Pittsburgh Steelers' mascot.

164. The Denver Broncos, mascot, Miles, was created on the same day as which Broncos, Super Bowl?

165. True or False: The Green Bay Packers' official mascot has the longest tenure of any mascot in the NFL.

166. What character served as the Cleveland Browns' logo before their logo became just a helmet in 1970?

167. In what year did the Cincinnati Bengals switch from the Bengal tiger logo to a striped "B" logo?

    a. 1970

    b. 1980

    c. 1990

    d. 2004

168. How many different logos have the Jacksonville Jaguars used since their creation?

169. From 1998 to 2018, the New York Jets' logo was a modified version of the '60s Jets' logo. Who was the coach that chose this modified version?

170. What did the New Orleans Saints model their logo after?

171. Is a seahawk a real bird?

172. Why are they called the Raiders?

173. Sir _____ is the name of the Carolina Panthers' mascot.

174. Who is the Chicago Bears' mascot, Staley Da Bear, named after?

175. _____ the Bull is the name of the Houston Texans' mascot.

176. How did the Green Bay Packers get their name?

177. What are buccaneers, and why is the Tampa, Florida, team named after them?

178. The Miami Dolphins' mascot is named T.D. What do the initials T.D. stand for?

179. The Cincinnati Bengals are named after Bengal tigers. Where are Bengal tigers from?

180. The New Orleans Saints have two mascots. One is a man named Sir Saint. What kind of animal is the other?

181. What was the original Tampa Bay Buccaneers' logo, which lasted from 1976 to 1996?

182. Why are the New York Jets called the Jets?

183. The 1966 Minnesota Vikings logo redesign changed the _____ of the emblem to signify looking toward the future.

184. Why is Philadelphia's team called the Eagles?

185. Why are the New York Giants called the Giants?

186. Which four NFL teams did not have a mascot during the 2023 season?

MOVES AND MERGERS

187. Which two NFL franchises were once traded for each other by their owners?

188. Which two NFL franchises played their first home games in Cleveland, Ohio?

189. During World War II, the Pittsburgh Steelers merged with two different franchises for one season each; which teams were they?

190. The AFL's Kansas City Chiefs played their first three seasons in what city?

191. The _____ are the only franchise to move to a new city more than once without ever returning to a city they previously resided in.

192. Which nine NFL franchises have their home stadium in a different city or state than the one in the team's name?

193. Which three NFL teams were moved into the newly formed AFC after the 1970 AFL merger?

194. What city did the Washington Commanders play in before moving in 1937?

195. These two franchises have each played "home" games in three different stadiums during the same season.

196. What city did the Detroit Lions originally play in, and what was their original franchise name?

FIELDS AND STADIUMS

197. What was the name of the Jacksonville Jaguars' stadium from 1996 to 2007?

198. What was the name of the Buffalo Bills' stadium from 1998 to 2015?

199. What was the first domed stadium in NFL history?

200. True or False: Soldier Field, home of the Chicago Bears, is the oldest stadium in the NFL.

201. Which team currently plays in Bank of America Stadium?

    a. Seattle Seahawks

    b. Carolina Panthers

    c. Arizona Cardinals

    d. Dallas Cowboys

202. Which team currently plays in a stadium named after their founder?

203. What year did Ford Field, home of the Detroit Lions, open?

204. _____ is the NFL stadium with the largest capacity.

205. What was the name of the stadium where the New England Patriots played from 1971 to 2001?

206. What was the name of the stadium where the Philadelphia Eagles played from 1971 to 2002?

207. True or False: The San Francisco 49ers played their final game in their old stadium, Candlestick Park, in 2013.

208. What did it cost to construct Lambeau Field (then named City Stadium) when it was built in 1957?

   a. $960,000

   b. $1.3 million

   c. $5.4 million

   d. $10.6 million

209. What year did the Miami Dolphins open up Hard Rock Stadium?

210. What stadium did the Indianapolis Colts play in from 1984 to 2007?

211. On what type of field do the Seattle Seahawks currently play?

212. _____ is the stadium with the smallest seating capacity in the NFL.

213. With a price tag of $1.9 billion, which stadium, which hosted Super Bowl LVIII (53) between the Kansas City Chiefs and the San Francisco 49ers, is the second-most expensive stadium in the world?

THE OWNER'S BOX

214. Who owns the Green Bay Packers?

215. What year did Jerry Jones become owner of the Dallas Cowboys?

216. True or False: John Mara and Steve Tisch are 50 percent co-owners of the New York Giants.

217. Which NFL owner was the first to have a net worth of over $15 billion?

    a. Jerry Jones

    b. Robert Kraft

    c. Stan Kroenke

    d. David Tepper

218. In what year did Jeffrey Lurie become the owner of the Philadelphia Eagles?

219. Which NFL owner is also the founder of the company Pilot Flying J?

220. In what year did Dan Snyder become owner of the Washington Commanders?

221. Which NFL owner was also a cofounder of Microsoft?

222. Which NFL owner was also once majority owner of the Denver Nuggets?

223. Which current NFL owner is known to have a legendary guitar collection?

224. True or False: Tennessee Titans owner Amy Strunk is the daughter of the founder of the team.

225. Who was the first female majority owner of an NFL team?

226. After which past NFL owner is the NFC championship trophy named?

227. After which past NFL owner is the AFC championship trophy named?

228. Match the NFL owner with the team they currently own or have owned:

1. Dean Spanos	a. Minnesota Vikings
2. David Tepper	b. Miami Dolphins
3. Steve Bisciotti	c. Los Angeles Chargers
4. Shahid Khan	d. Carolina Panthers
5. Zygi Wilf	e. Baltimore Ravens
6. Stephen M. Ross	f. Jacksonville Jaguars

229. Which eccentric businessman became the owner of the Las Vegas Raiders in 2011?

230. Sold in 2022 for a record price tag of $4.65 billion, which team was purchased by an investment group led by Walmart heir Rob Walton?

NOW-DEFUNCT NFL TEAMS

In the early 1920s, what today's football fans know as the National Football League was called the American Professional Football Association (APFA). Some of the franchises from those early days won the league's first few championships, including the Hammond Pros, who won a title even though their title game ended in a scoreless tie. (They were awarded the title due to having the better regular season record.)

One of those early teams was the Akron Pros, who won the 1920 APFA championship with an 8–0–3 record. Akron's biggest claim to fame happened in 1920, when Fritz Pollard joined the Pros, making him the first Black player (and first Black head coach a year later) in league history and earning a spot in the Pro Football Hall of Fame.

Canton, Ohio, saw what is considered the first NFL dynasty when, from 1921 to 1923, the Canton Bulldogs went 25 straight games without losing, for a record of 22–0–3. They are credited with winning the first two NFL titles in 1922 and 1923 and were led by Jim Thorpe, the first Native American to win an Olympic Gold Medal for the United States. Thorpe also served as the league's president in his first season.

Despite their on-field success, the Canton Bulldogs struggled financially and were sold after the 1923 season. Their best players joined the best players from the Cleveland Indians football team to form the Cleveland Bulldogs, who went on to win the 1924 championship with a 7–0–1 record.

> continues

Money issues troubled the franchise, though, and before the end of the decade, they were history.

In 1926, football fans would need to go to northern Philadelphia to watch the NFL champions play. That season, the Frankford Yellow Jackets posted a 14–1–2 record, and the 14 wins would stand as an NFL record until 1984, when the San Francisco 49ers went 15–1 during the regular season.

The NFL reached Rhode Island in 1925, when the Providence Steam Rollers—a semipro team founded in 1916—were invited to join the league. Despite very low financial resources—which led to each player being issued only one uniform for the entire season—the Steam Rollers won the 1928 NFL championship. The franchise peaked that season, but after they hosted the first night game in NFL history in October 1929, the Great Depression would cost the team fans and money. By the end of the 1931 season, the last major professional sports team to call Rhode Island home returned to its origins as a semipro football team.

CHAPTER 3

PLAYERS

NFL players are the lifeblood of the NFL. Whether the player is a future Hall of Famer, All-Pro, Pro Bowler, or just a "role player," all players make the NFL exciting to watch. Now, there is a huge difference between being just a "role player" and being a great player, and it all starts with how they see the field and how they perform when the time comes. Great players are those who consistently rise to the occasion and perform, and who know how to make other players around them better. Great players are those who have a long career in a sport where "long" and "career" don't go together. And great players are those who you will pay to see, whether you root for or against them. Think Tom Brady: a player who consistently rose to the occasion and knew how to make those around him better, whether it was when leading the Patriots to multiple Super Bowl wins or joining the Buccaneers and changing the team's culture overnight to help them win a Super Bowl—but also someone that opposing teams loved to beat because of who he is. That's a great player.

NAME THAT PLAYER

231. For the first time, in 2004, which two high school teammates both received Heisman Trophy votes?

232. Which San Diego Chargers tight end finished his NFL career with 11,841 receiving yards—63 less than Hall of Famer Michael Irvin—despite having never played a single game of college football?

233. Which two Super Bowl MVP quarterbacks attended the same Texas high school eight years apart?

234. Who was the first cornerback to win Super Bowl MVP?

235. Which Pittsburgh Steelers wide receiver never won a Super Bowl MVP?

    a.   Santonio Homes

    b.   John Stallworth

    c.   Lynn Swann

    d.   Hines Ward

236. Which quarterback won the Super Bowl MVP despite throwing for only 119 yards in the game?

237. Which player is the only Pro Football Hall of Famer who attended the University of New Mexico?

238. How many touchdowns did Chicago Bears running back Walter Payton score in Super Bowl XX (20)?

239. There have been 21 players to record four interceptions in one game, but only three players since 1986. Which three players had four interceptions in the same game between 1986 and 2020?

240. Name the first two players to ever play in and win back-to-back Super Bowl titles with different teams?

241. What player is the all-time leading scorer among players who spent their entire career with one franchise?

242. Who was the first player in NFL history to score 20 return touchdowns?

243. Who holds the record for the longest kickoff return without scoring a touchdown?

244. Who is the only Hall of Famer to wear 59 on his NFL jersey?

245. Name the only player to reach the Pro Bowl playing three different positions.

246. Which running back holds the record for the most career season rushing titles?

247. Rank these quarterbacks by their total career passing yards:

    a.   Kerry Collins

    b.   Dan Fouts

    c.   Joe Montana

    d.   Vinny Testaverde

248. What outside linebacker from the 2010s All-Decade Team spends his off-season on his own commercial poultry farm?

249. What Super Bowl–winning placekicker is also an opera singer and can sing in seven languages?

250. Name the only kicker to win the NFL's MVP award.

251. Name the All-Pro NFL quarterback who went to the same high school as Barry Bonds.

252. Name the first quarterback to win a Super Bowl with two different teams.

253. Name the first player to rush for 1,000 yards and record 100 receptions in the same season.

254. Who was the first left-handed quarterback to make the Hall of Fame?

255. Name the only two quarterbacks to have thrown for 500+ passing yards in a playoff game.

256. Name the only quarterback to have thrown for 500+ passing yards in three regular season games.

257. Name the only NFL kicker to record a 66-yard field goal.

258. Name the NFL player that recorded the most rushing yards in a single game.

259. Steve Young, Tom Brady, and _____ are the only quarterbacks to throw for six touchdowns in a single playoff game.

260. Name the NFL player with the most receptions in a single game.

261. Name the only running back to have six rushing touchdowns in a single game.

262. _____ holds the record for most receiving yards in a single game.

263. _____ holds the record for most receiving yards in a single playoff game.

264. Who holds the record for most sacks in a single game?

265. _____ holds the record for most sacks in a single play-off game.

266. Who holds the record for most solo tackles in a single game?

267. Who holds the record for most solo tackles in a single season?

268. _____ holds the record for most sacks in a career.

269. Minnesota Vikings safety Paul Krause, New York Giants safety Emlen Tunnell, and _____ are the only NFL players to end their careers with over 70 interceptions.

270. Who were the only two NFL players to win the NFL MVP award unanimously?

271. This player is not only known for being one of the greatest receivers in NFL history, but also for his antics, which include being recorded saying he pays his fines in cash instead of checks.

272. _____ made headlines for his off-the-field behavior during his team's Super Bowl media appearances when he answered every question by explaining he only appeared to avoid a fine.

273. This player is known not only for being one of the greatest tight ends, but also for a game against the Patriots in which he acted like he was calling the president and was requesting help for the Patriots during a blowout game.

274. _____ is the first to ever win Defensive Player of the Year in his rookie season.

275. This player's antics included prank calling his coaches at 2:00 a.m. just to let them know he was open.

276. Who is the first player to ever rush for over 10,000 yards?

277. This quarterback delayed his entry into the NFL for four years due to military commitments after graduating from the U.S. Naval Academy.

278. Who was the first player to ever have multiple 20-sack seasons?

279. This player is the first to record two seasons of 1,600 yards receiving in NFL history.

280. Name the player who was the first ever to record seven sacks in a single game.

281. In 2023, Patrick Mahomes became the third quarterback to have multiple 5,000-yard passing seasons. Who were the other two?

282. In 2022, Lamar Jackson eclipsed this player's record for the most 100-yard rushing games by a quarterback.

283. Who set the record for the most career kickoff returns for touchdowns in 2022?

284. Which quarterback was officially traded to the Denver Broncos in 2023 in a blockbuster move that involved three players and four draft picks?

285. Which quarterback signed a five-year, $230 million fully guaranteed contract with the Cleveland Browns in 2023?

INNOVATORS

286. What 1997 rule change was named after Cowboys running back Emmitt Smith?

287. What 1979 rule change made it harder for running backs to be effective and was named after a former Cleveland Browns running back?

288. What rule change was made in 2009 and is informally named after former Steelers wide receiver Hines Ward?

289. What 1981 rule was created in large part due to former Raiders cornerback Lester Hayes?

290. Name the two Pro Bowl wide receivers who influenced the revision of the "standard for a catch" in 2018, which led to the elimination of "surviving the ground" during a catch?

291. Which NFL rule was enhanced and called more tightly in 2018 after Green Bay Packers quarterback Aaron Rodgers suffered a broken collarbone?

292. This Hall of Fame cornerback is "credited" with forcing the NFL to add the "one chuck" rule during pass plays.

293. When running back Bronko Nagurski of the Chicago Bears threw a pass to running back Red Grange in a 1932 playoff game, it caused a rule change that is still in effect today. What was the new rule?

294. In 1978, which restriction on offensive linemen was removed, making it easier to pass block?

295. Which famous play from 1972 forced the NFL to make "tip drills" legal during games?

296. What rule was added after the 1978 "Holy Roller" play between the Oakland Raiders and San Diego Chargers?

297. Which Hall of Fame cornerback is largely responsible for the NFL prohibiting the grabbing of the facemask?

298. Which Hall of Fame defensive end is responsible for the creation of the "Head Slap Rule"?

299. Which Pro Bowl quarterback suffered an ACL injury in 2005 that led to the NFL implementing a rule that prevents defensive players from hitting quarterbacks at or below the knee?

300. Which rule change is named after Kansas City Chiefs tight end Morris Stroud?

301. Which rule change is named after Cleveland Browns kicker Phil Dawson?

302. Which NFL safety is largely responsible for the banning of the horse-collar tackle?

303. Who was the first quarterback to throw for 500 or more passing yards in a single game?

304. Which NFL rule is named after Miami Dolphins running back Ricky Williams?

305. What rule change is named after New England Patriots cornerback Ty Law?

UNBELIEVABLE PLAYS

306. Which player is known for making a helmet catch in Super Bowl XLII (42)?

307. Which player is known for making a goal line interception to seal Super Bowl XLIX (49)?

308. Which player is known for making the catch during the "Philly Special" play?

309. Which player is known for "The Catch"?

310. Which player is known for "The Immaculate Reception"?

311. Which player is known for making an interception after the offense called a play known as "Red Right 88"?

312. Which quarterback is known for converting "4th and 26"?

    a.   Patrick Mahomes

    b.   Brett Favre

    c.   Donovan McNabb

    d.   John Elway

313. Which player is known for the "Butt Fumble"?

314. Which Miami Dolphins player is known for scoring the game-winning touchdown in "The Miami Miracle"?

315. Which quarterback is known for calling a fake spike to beat the New York Jets?

    a.   Tom Brady

    b.   Dan Marino

    c.   Peyton Manning

    d.   Jim Kelly

316. Which player is known for "The Miracle at the New Meadowlands"?

317. Which player is known for sacrificing his body with a helicopter spin to secure a first down in a Super Bowl?

318. Which player is "Ghost" in the play called "Ghost to the Post"?

319. Which wide receiver is known for "The Catch 2"?

320. _____ is known for making the "Sea of Hands" catch in an AFC divisional playoff game.

321. Which player is well known for making a ridiculous fingertip catch against the Dallas Cowboys?

322. Which player is known for making the catch and scoring during the "Minneapolis Miracle"?

323. Which player is known for making a ridiculous catch in Super Bowl LI (51), where he caught the football over two defensive players and a third defensive player's legs?

324. Which quarterback became known for the Hail Mary pass?

325. Which player is known for scoring during the "Music City Miracle"?

FEUDS

326. Terrell Owens has openly criticized a former teammate and blames said teammate for his one Super Bowl loss, as well as the reason he was let go by the team they both were on. Who is the teammate?

327. Name the NFL player that Odell Beckham Jr. got into a feud with and famously launched himself at during a game that included five personal fouls between the two players.

328. Name the NFL player that Andre Johnson famously fought on the football field.

329. Which NFL player threatened to retire after winning an MVP due to his distrust of his team's GM and front office?

330. Name the NFL player who was traded to the Raiders, yet never played a game with the team due to him forcing his release.

331. Name the NFL player that Rob Gronkowski famously "threw out of the club" during a game because he was running his mouth too much.

332. Name the NFL player that Richard Sherman famously called a "sorry receiver" after the NFC Championship Game.

333. Name the NFL player that famously didn't like Tom Brady and referenced his "smug attitude" as one of the reasons.

334. Name the NFL player that had repeated run-ins with head coach Jon Gruden, which famously led to his deactivation for the final six games of the 2003 season.

335. Who is the NFL player that Peyton Manning had an issue with after that player blamed Manning for the Colts 2002 Wildcard playoff loss to the New York Jets?

336. Which star 1980s running back was called "a cancer to the team" by Raiders owner Al Davis during a feud between them?

MOONLIGHTING

337. Which NFL cornerback was drafted by the Atlanta Falcons and also played for the New York Yankees during his career?

338. _____ played for the Kansas City Royals before joining the NFL and playing running back for the Los Angeles Raiders.

339. Name the NFL player who won a Heisman Trophy, started at quarterback in the NFL, and played for the New York Mets.

340. True or False: Quarterback Russell Wilson was the Colorado Rockies' first round pick in 2010.

341. True or False: Quarterback Tom Brady was the Montreal Expos' 18th round draft pick in 1995.

342. Name the defensive back who played for the Atlanta Hawks for three years before leaving the NFL to play for the St. Louis Cardinals for 15 years.

343. After playing in the NFL since 2011, this wide receiver played professional lacrosse for the Cannons Lacrosse Club in 2021. Who is the player?

   a. T. J. Yates

   b. Gabe Miller

   c. Chris Hogan

   d. Johnny White

344. Name the player that was the Miami Marlins' second-round draft pick in 1992 and threw the very first pitch in the history of their franchise before playing in the NFL and becoming a Hall of Famer.

345. Which running back played for the Miami Dolphins and was drafted by the Philadelphia Phillies in 1995?

346. Name the quarterback who played for the New York Yankees and later the Dallas Cowboys.

347. Which Colts tight end is the all-time leader in field goal percentage for the Virginia Commonwealth University Rams?

WHO SAID IT?

348. Which NFL player said this: "I love me some me"?

349. Which NFL player said this: "You don't have to win it. Just don't lose it"?

350. _____ once said, "I may be dumb, but I'm not stupid."

351. Which NFL player said this: "I feel like I'm the best, but you're not going to get me to say that"?

352. Which NFL player is known for telling a cornerback to "ice up, son"?

353. Which NFL player said this: "If you look good, you feel good; if you feel good, you play good; if you play good, they pay good"?

354. _____ once said, "I don't know whether I prefer Astroturf to grass. I never smoked Astroturf."

355. Which NFL player said this: "Yo soy fiesta"?

356. _____ once said, "I've been big ever since I was little."

357. Which NFL player said this: "Nobody in football should be called a genius. A genius is a guy like Norman Einstein"?

358. Which NFL player famously said, "I like to believe that my best hits border on felonious assault"?

359. _____ once said, "I wouldn't ever set out to hurt anyone deliberately unless it was, you know, important—like a league game or something."

360. Which NFL player famously said, "I don't give players a chance to hit me"?

361. Which NFL player said, "There is no defense against a perfect pass. I can throw the perfect pass"?

362. Which NFL player famously said, "You wanna know which ring is my favorite? The next one"?

363. Which NFL player said, "I'm just here so I won't get fined," during a postgame press conference?

364. Which San Francisco 49er sarcastically said, "Yeah, I suck. Everybody else on the team scored, except for me," after his 17-game touchdown streak was snapped in 2023?

WHEN PLAYERS GO HOLLYWOOD

For generations, the exposure NFL players received has helped some of them find work on the small or big screen after their playing days were over. Here are some former NFL players who made it big in Hollywood after hanging up their pads and cleats.

Carl Weathers: It would be difficult to imagine the *Rocky* movies having the success they did in the late 1970s without the character of Apollo Creed. Creed was played by Carl Weathers, a former college football standout at San Diego State who played two seasons at linebacker for the Oakland Raiders before giving up football for an acting career. Younger fans might also know Weathers from his role as Greef Karga in *The Mandalorian*.

Michael Strahan: One of the NFL's greatest defensive ends would also turn his attention to Hollywood a year after he retired. Michael Strahan, a beloved New York Giants player and Hall of Famer, retired in 2008 and the following year landed a lead role in *Brothers*, a TV sitcom on Fox. The show had poor ratings and lasted only a single season, but Strahan did all right for himself, moving on to multiple morning show hosting gigs.

Howie Long: Here is an NFL player who took the fearlessness he showed on the NFL field to the big screen. After he retired following the 1993 NFL season, Long pursued a new career in acting, beginning with starring in the 1998 film *Firestorm*. Even though that film was a box office flop, Long

> continues

continued to find roles in movies such as *Broken Arrow* and *3000 Miles to Graceland*.

Bubba Smith: There is something about NFL defensive ends trying to make it big in Hollywood after their NFL careers are over. That's because we have Bubba Smith, the first overall pick by the Baltimore Colts from the 1967 Draft. Smith was a two-time Pro Bowler at defensive end before retiring at 31 to take up acting. He became known for his work in the *Police Academy* films as Moses Hightower, a befitting name for the 6'7" athlete with the strength to match his size. He left the NFL with 52.5 career sacks.

Merlin Olsen: One of the NFL's best players also became one of its best broadcasters and a television star. Merlin Olsen was a 14-time Pro Bowl defensive tackle with the Los Angeles Rams from 1962 to 1976, during which time he earned his reputation as the one of the best to play the position. After he retired, he appeared on four seasons of *Little House on the Prairie* as Jonathan Garvey, and later joined NBC Sports as a color commentator for NFL games.

Fred Dryer: Another NFL player who found huge success on the small screen was Fred Dryer, a 1969 first-round draft pick of the New York Giants who played three seasons with them as a defensive end before joining the Los Angeles Rams for 10 years. A few years after his retirement in 1981, Dryer landed the role of Sgt. Rick Hunter in *Hunter*. The show ran from 1984 to 1991 and was seen in as many as 88 countries through syndication.

Jim Brown: One trailblazer among NFL players turning to Hollywood for their next job was Jim Brown, who dominated the game at running back before walking away from the Cleveland Browns in 1965 at age 29. In 1967, *The Dirty Dozen* was released, giving Brown a new avenue of opportunity and opening the door for future athletes who had box office appeal. Two decades later, Brown was still on the silver screen in films like *The Running Man* and *Any Given Sunday*, proving that his staying power wasn't limited to those who saw him on the gridiron.

CHAPTER 4

COACHES

From intimidator to motivator, the job of an NFL head coach has evolved over time. The era of no-nonsense coaches like Vince Lombardi of the Green Bay Packers created the first NFL dynasty of the Super Bowl era. From there, the counterculture of the Oakland Raiders was born when their head coach, John Madden, let his players do what they wanted from Monday to Saturday as long as they showed up and performed on Sunday. Next came the intellectual head coaching style of Bill Walsh, who created the West Coast offense for the San Francisco 49ers, a scheme still used in many forms decades later. Each style comes in and out of fashion, with Bill Parcells and Bill Belichick reminding many of Lombardi, while Jimmy Johnson followed in the footsteps of John Madden. All of these coaches have one thing in common, though: success, something that never goes out of style.

NAME THAT COACH

365. Which Super Bowl–winning linebacker became interim head coach of the Las Vegas Raiders and led the team to a 5-4 record to close the 2023 season?

366. Which Cleveland Browns head coach became the first since 2015 to win games with four different quarterbacks (Deshaun Watson, PJ Walker, Dorian Thompson-Robinson, and Joe Flacco) in one season?

367. Which NFL coach has the highest all-time winning percentage in the playoffs, with a minimum of 10 games played?

368. From 1960 to 2020, which NFL coach had the most regular season wins of all time?

369. Who was the first coach to win 100 games with two different teams?

370. Who was the first Black NFL head coach to win a Super Bowl?

371. Which NFL coach was the first to win four NFL Coach of the Year awards?

    a. Bill Belichick

    b. Don Shula

    c. Vince Lombardi

    d. George Halas

372. Which NFL head coach has the most Super Bowl wins?

373. From 1960 to 2020, which NFL coach had the most consecutive winning seasons?

374. Who was the New York Giants head coach that defeated the previously undefeated New England Patriots in Super Bowl XLII (42)?

375. Which NFL coach has had the longest tenure of any head coach in NFL history?

376. From 1960 to 2020, which NFL head coach had coached in the most playoff games?

377. Name the first NFL head coach to go undefeated and win the Super Bowl during the same season.

378. Who was the first NFL head coach to win more than one Super Bowl?

379. From 1967 to 2024, who are the two NFL head coaches to win at least four Super Bowls?

380. Who was the first Black NFL head coach?

381. Which NFL coach invented the West Coast offense?

382. Which NFL coach invented the 4–3 defense?

383. From 1960 to 2020, who was the oldest person to serve as head coach in an NFL game?

384. Which former NFL coach won the Walter Payton NFL Man of the Year award?

385. _____ and the Miami Dolphins' Don Shula are the first two NFL head coaches to reach 300+ wins.

386. From 1967 to 2020, which NFL head coach had the highest regular season winning percentage?

   a.   Bill Belichick

   b.   Don Shula

   c.   John Madden

   d.   Bill Walsh

387. Which NFL head coach won the Coach of the Year award in 1986 and again in 1994?

388. Who was the last NFL head coach to win the Coach of the Year award in back-to-back seasons?

389. Which NFL head coach is 4–0 in Super Bowl appearances?

390. This NFL coach played quarterback for two arena football teams in the 1980s.

391. Who was the first NFL head coach to bring two different franchises to three consecutive conference championships each?

392. Who was the first NFL head coach to win at least one playoff game in his first four seasons?

393. Who was the first NFL head coach to win three Super Bowls with three different quarterbacks?

394. Bill Parcells and _____, widely regarded as the very first coaches to be doused with Gatorade after a big win, both received Gatorade baths on October 28, 1984.

395. _____ was the first NFL coach to win a Super Bowl as a player, an assistant coach, and a head coach.

396. Who was the first NFL head coach to win a Super Bowl and a College Football Playoff National Championship?

397. This head coach was known as "Papa Bear."

398. _____ and _____ were the first siblings to face off as head coaches in the Super Bowl.

399. Who was the first NFL head coach to win a division title with three different teams?

400. Name the two NFL coaches suspended for the entire 2012 season due to their involvement in the New Orleans Saints' Bountygate scandal?

401. Who was the youngest head coach in NFL history?

402. Which NFL head coach was known for wearing a fedora during every game he coached in?

403. Who was the only NFL head coach to lead four different teams to the playoffs?

404. _____ has the most wins of any head coach who never won an NFL championship.

405. Name the New York Jets strength and conditioning coach who was suspended for tripping an opposing player mid play.

406. Marty Schottenheimer and _____ are the only NFL coaches to open their head coaching career with 14 straight non-losing seasons.

407. Name the Denver Broncos head coach who resigned after the 1976 season after failing to make the playoffs during his five-year tenure.

408. In the early part of the 1978 NFL season, who took over as head coach of the San Diego Chargers after Tommy Prothro abruptly resigned?

409. Name the head coach whose team won the Super Bowl and was named Coach of the Year in 1999, then retired immediately afterward.

410. Name the Buffalo Bills head coach who was fired midseason after coaching the team for only 21 games?

411. Who was the first Black head coach of the Chicago Bears?

412. Who did the Indianapolis Colts select as interim head coach in the middle of the 2022 season, despite the person having no coaching experience?

413. Who became just the fifth head coach in NFL history to not complete his first season, after being fired by the Denver Broncos?

414. Name the four NFL coaches who have won both a college football national championship and a Super Bowl.

415. Which Super Bowl-winning coach turned legendary commentator said, "If you have two quarterbacks, you actually have none"?

COACHING TREES

416. Name the legendary head coach who served as New York Giants head coach Bill Parcells's defensive coordinator during the years he won Super Bowl XXI (21) and XXV (25).

417. Which Super Bowl–winning head coach once worked under New York Giants head coach Bill Parcells as his offensive coordinator?

418. Name the four Super Bowl–winning head coaches who worked under Kansas City Chiefs head coach Marty Schottenheimer.

419. Three NFL coaches who have worked under Tony Dungy in the past that have either made or won Super Bowls as the head coach of their own team. Name these three head coaches.

420. Which coach, who worked under Pittsburgh Steelers head coach Bill Cowher, is widely considered one of the greatest defensive coordinators of all time?

421. Which former Arizona Cardinals head coach had both of his twin sons on his coaching staff?

422. Which legendary college football coach worked under Bill Belichick as a defensive coordinator with the Cleveland Browns?

423. Name the father and son who were the head coach and offensive coordinator of the Washington Commanders at the same time.

424. Dallas Cowboys head coach Tom Landry's coaching tree has only won a single Super Bowl. Who is the coach that won the Super Bowl?

425. Which two NFL head coaches that worked under Mike Shanahan went to the Super Bowl in back-to-back years of each other and lost?

426. Name the two NFL head coaches who have won a Super Bowl and who came from Mike Holmgren's coaching tree.

427. Who is the NFL coach that worked under Andy Reid as a special teams coordinator and later won a Super Bowl as a head coach for the Baltimore Ravens?

428. Name the father-son coaching duo that worked together with the Houston Oilers and then the New Orleans Saints.

429. Which legendary coaching tree did San Francisco 49ers head coach Bill Walsh come from?

   a. Tom Landry's

   b. Paul Brown's

   c. George Halas's

   d. Vince Lombardi's

430. Name the two former NFL head coaches who have won a Super Bowl and who came from Bill Walsh's coaching tree.

431. Which coaching tree did Buffalo Bills head coach Sean McDermott originate from?

   a. Bill Belichick

   b. Andy Reid

   c. Bill Cowher

   d. Tony Dungy

432. Which coaching tree did former Arizona Cardinals head coach Dennis Green originate from?

433. Which coaching tree did former Philadelphia Eagles head coach Ray Rhodes originate from?

434. Which coaching tree did Washington Commanders head coach Ron Rivera originate from?

435. Which Super Bowl–winning head coach once worked under Los Angeles Rams head coach George Allen as his special teams coordinator?

INNOVATORS

436. What play—created by head coach Bill Belichick and offensive coordinator Josh McDaniels in the 2014 playoffs—prompted the league to institute a rule that made it illegal for offensive players with eligible jerseys to report that they were ineligible receivers?

437. What 2008 rule helped the defensive side of the ball and was formed, in large part, due to Bill Belichick and the Spygate scandal?

438. Which legendary NFL coach was one of the first to declare that he would not tolerate players who harbored racial prejudices?

439. Who was the first NFL coach to hire a woman to his coaching squad?

440. Which NFL coach introduced the no-huddle/hurry-up offense to the NFL?

441. Which coach introduced pro football to the idea of studying and breaking down film?

442. Name the two NFL coaches that together created the Tampa 2 Defense.

443. Who was the first NFL coach to draft an openly gay player?

444. Which NFL coach came up with the idea for a single-bar face mask to protect players?

445. Which NFL coach introduced Gatorade to the NFL as a way to keep players hydrated?

446. Which coach was the defensive coordinator who created the 46 defense, which helped the Chicago Bears post a 15-1 record during the 1985 season?

FEUDS

447. Name the player that New England Patriots offensive coordinator Bill O'Brien famously got into a shouting match with after said player was telling a teammate what he did wrong on a play.

448. Who did head coach Jimmy Johnson famously have a feud with over the share of credit given for the Cowboys dynasty, which led to his departure from the Dallas Cowboys?

449. Former 49ers head coach Jim Harbaugh famously got into a postgame dispute with a coach over the way the coach gave him a handshake. Who was the coach?

   a.   Bill Belichick

   b.   Rex Ryan

   c.   Pete Carroll

   d.   Jim Schwartz

450. Name the coach that New England Patriots head coach Bill Belichick has been in a years-long feud with over the first coach reporting him to the NFL for Spygate.

451. Who did Bill Parcells famously get into a dispute with over that person interfering with player personnel decisions?

452. Name the coach that Chicago Bears head coach Mike Ditka famously feuded with over "creative differences," and who was also part of Dikta's staff at one point.

453. Which NFL owner did head coach Mike Shanahan famously get into a feud with over his micromanaging, which ultimately led to Shanahan's firing?

454. Name the coach that Buddy Ryan famously punched during the 1993 NFL season over the coach's use of the run-and-shoot offense while working on the same staff as Ryan.

455. Name the coach that Denver Broncos head coach Dan Reeves famously feuded with and ultimately fired after the 1991 NFL season due to insubordination.

456. Former Cincinnati Bengals head coach Sam Wyche feuded with a Houston Oilers head coach for years over insults and in-game cheap shots to players, called that coach a "phony," and famously blew out that coach's team 61–7. Who was the coach?

WHO SAID IT

457. Which NFL coach said, "Cannot play with them, cannot win with them, cannot coach with them. Can't do it. I want winners. I want people that want to win"?

458. Which NFL coach famously said, "We're the dumbest team in America"?

   a. Bill Belichick

   b. Bill Parcells

   c. Bill Callahan

   d. Mike Ditka

459. Which NFL coach said, "They are who we thought they were. And we let them off the hook"?

460. Which NFL coach said, "You play to win the game. You don't play it to just play it"?

461. Which NFL coach famously said, "Playoffs?! Don't talk about playoffs! Are you kidding me? Playoffs?! I just hope we can win a game"?

462. Which NFL coach famously said, "If they want you to cook the dinner, at least they ought to let you shop for some of the groceries"?

   a. Mike Ditka

   b. Bill Parcells

   c. Rex Ryan

   d. Nick Saban

463. Which NFL coach famously said, "I don't Twitter, I don't MyFace, I don't Yearbook"?

   a. Bill Belichick

   b. Bruce Arians

   c. Mike Tomlin

   d. Andy Reid

464. _____ said, "We didn't tackle well today but we made up for it by not blocking."

465. Which NFL coach said, "Stats are for losers; final scores are for winners"?

466. Which NFL coach said, "If you take a swipe at one of ours, we'll take two swipes at one of yours. We're going to turn the heat up, we're going to let the fur fly, and let's see what happens"?

   a. Dan Campbell

   b. Rex Ryan

   c. Mike Vrabel

   d. Jon Gruden

467. Which NFL coach said, "The road to easy street goes through the sewer"?

    a. John Madden

    b. Andy Reid

    c. Pete Carroll

    d. Vince Lombardi

468. Which NFL coach hilariously said, "I don't think there's anybody in this organization not focused on the 49ers ... I mean the Chargers"?

    a. John Mckay

    b. Rex Ryan

    c. John Madden

    d. Bill Belichick

469. _____ said, "You guys line up alphabetically by height."

470. Which NFL coach said, "We can't run. We can't pass. We can't stop the run. We can't stop the pass. We can't kick. Other than that, we're just not a very good football team right now"?

471. _____ said, "My wife wishes I had DeMarcus Ware's body."

472. When discussing his knack for going for it on fourth down, which head coach said, "Here's what I would say, because I tell my family this, 'Just wear a diaper before some of these games.' I'll give them an alert and say, 'Put them on and be ready to roll.'"

473. Name the longtime Seahawks coach who was fired in 2024.

474. Which embattled New York coach said prior to the start of the 2023 season, "If you ain't got no haters, you ain't popping. So hate away"?

HEAD COACHES TURNED BROADCASTERS

NFL head coaches have always provided some of the best entertainment in sports. It's no wonder why networks have put microphones on them during games and even lured some of them into the broadcasting booth to call games.

John Madden: John Madden is a Hall of Fame head coach. Some only know him as a broadcaster and the name on their favorite video game. Madden was paired for many years with Pat Summerall, also a former NFL player, and the two fit together like a hand and a glove. Summerall would provide the play-by-play for color commentary by Madden, who was known to get so excited that he would speak a new language made up of sounds rather than words. Somehow it all made perfect sense to those watching the game.

Hank Stram: The colorful head coach of the Kansas City Chiefs often provided wonderful in-game commentary when wearing an NFL Films microphone. When paired with such broadcasters as Jack Buck, Vin Sully, and Sean McDonough, Stram spoke to the fans as a fan himself, very plainly and passionately.

Tony Dungy: Sunday Night Football gained a wealth of football knowledge when they added Tony Dungy to their pregame show as a color analyst. The calm, cool, and collected head coach always prioritized his faith and family in the NFL, and was able to show his coaching peers that a coach can be successful through teaching and guiding players instead of yelling and belittling. Dungy is a calming presence, whether speaking to his partners on the set or to the fans watching at home.

CHAPTER 5

SUPER BOWL

As the only truly undisputed national sports holiday,
Super Bowl Sunday is a day when, since the 1970s, at least
a quarter of the United States and many more people
around the world sit down to watch the final game of the
National Football League season. Some watch because
this is the game where an average Joe can be turned into
a hero for their team and forever be known as a key player
in a Super Bowl championship. Other players, however,
can see their career fall into ruin, never able to recover
from having a bad game during the biggest moment of
their career.

This is also the rare television show that brings in
as many viewers to watch the commercials as the main
attraction. Additionally, the NFL has made the Super Bowl
halftime show an event unto itself, with fans winning a
chance to be on the field for those 15 minutes, and many
more just tuning in to watch whichever megastar takes
the stage.

MEMORABLE MOMENTS

475. Which Super Bowl–winning head coach called for an onside kick to begin the second half?

    a. Bruce Arians

    b. Sean Payton

    c. John Harbaugh

    d. Bill Belichick

476. Which kick returner became the first player to return the opening Super Bowl kickoff for a touchdown?

477. Which franchise holds the record for the most points scored in a quarter during the Super Bowl?

478. Which states with NFL teams have hosted the Super Bowl only once?

479. How long was the field goal, missed by Buffalo Bills kicker Scott Norwood, to end Super Bowl XXV (25)?

480. Who were the wide receiver and linebacker involved in the "One Yard Short" tackle of Super Bowl XXXIV (34)?

481. Which two teams saw the lights go out during their Super Bowl?

482. Which kicker almost "threw away" the Miami Dolphins' perfect 17–0 season in Super Bowl VII (7)?

483. Which placekicker tied the Super Bowl with a late-game field goal before making a mistake on the ensuing kickoff that contributed to his team losing the championship?

484. Whose sprint down the Rose Bowl field and subsequent ball strip in Super Bowl XXVII (27) took away a touchdown from the Dallas Cowboys' Leon Lett?

485. Which Seattle Seahawks wide receiver was the intended target of a pass from quarterback Russell Wilson, which was intercepted by cornerback Malcolm Butler to seal the New England Patriots' win in Super Bowl XLIX (49)?

486. In Super Bowl XLIII (43), this linebacker intercepted future Hall of Fame quarterback Kurt Warner on the final play of the first half and scored a touchdown as time expired.

487. Who scored the first touchdown in Super Bowl history?

488. Which two wideouts were on the receiving end of quarterback Eli Manning's two famous Super Bowl passes?

489. Which two Pittsburgh Steelers wide receivers teamed up on a touchdown pass to seal their Super Bowl XL (40) win over the Seattle Seahawks?

490. Which Super Bowl was the first to be played on artificial turf?

491. Which actor became part of Super Bowl lore after being pointed out by a player on the field?

492. Which two teammates are the only ones to score three touchdowns each in the same Super Bowl?

493. Which future Hall of Famer was looking for his helmet at the start of one of his Super Bowl appearances?

494. Which team carried both their head coach and defensive coordinator off the field after a dominating Super Bowl victory?

495. Name the three players who were all part of the "Philly Special" in Super Bowl LII (52).

496. Who scored the first overtime touchdown in Super Bowl history?

497. Which cornerback ended a potential game-tying drive by Indianapolis Colts quarterback Peyton Manning with a pick-six, ensuring the New Orleans Saints' first-ever Super Bowl victory?

498. Which two players returned back-to-back kickoffs for touchdowns in Super Bowl XXXV (35)?

499. Which head coach allowed an opponent to score a tiebreaking touchdown before going on to lose the same Super Bowl when a comeback effort failed?

500. Which Dallas Cowboys tight end dropped a game-tying touchdown pass in the end zone during a four-point loss to the Pittsburgh Steelers in Super Bowl XIII (13)?

501. Which placekicker was the first to win a Super Bowl with a last-second field goal?

502. Which "appliance" scored a rushing touchdown during Super Bowl XX (20)?

503. A fourth-and-one touchdown by which running back helped the Washington Commanders win Super Bowl XVII (17)?

504. Which quarterback is famous for running off the field with one finger raised into the air in victory?

505. What broadcaster was proven wrong by the New England Patriots after saying the team should play for overtime rather than the win?

506. Which quarterback was reportedly sick in the team's huddle, preventing a potential game-winning touchdown drive against the New England Patriots?

507. Which team helped secure their first Super Bowl victory with a four-play goal line stand considered one of the best in NFL history?

508. Which Super Bowl–winning head coach was once carried off the field by a fan, not his players?

509. Who was the first Super Bowl player to say, "I'm going to Disney World" after the game?

510. Which players became the first set of brothers to face each other, in the 2023 Super Bowl?

RECORD HOLDERS

511. Which running back holds the record with three rushing touchdowns in a Super Bowl?

512. Who is the only player to score three touchdowns in two different Super Bowls?

513. Which running back holds the record for the most rushing yards in the Super Bowl?

514. Which running back is the only one to average over 10 yards per carry in the Super Bowl?

515. Who holds the record for the most interceptions thrown in a single Super Bowl?

516. Which quarterback has thrown the most career Super Bowl interceptions?

517. Which player was on a record five Super Bowl–losing teams?

518. Which player holds the record for the most consecutive Super Bowls wins?

519. Which head coach holds the Super Bowl record for the most wins with different starting quarterbacks?

520. Kickers Jim Turner (New York Jets) and Mike Clark (Dallas Cowboys) are tied for a Super Bowl record that can never be broken. What is that record?

521. Which defender holds the record for the most quarterback sacks in a single Super Bowl?

522. Which defensive star was the first to win five Super Bowls during his Hall of Fame career?

523. Which San Francisco 49er very briefly held the record for the longest field goal in Super Bowl history, before being beat by the opposing team's kicker in the same game?

524. Who was the first starting quarterback to ever win a Super Bowl at age 23?

   a. Tom Brady

   b. Patrick Mahomes

   c. Russell Wilson

   d. Ben Roethlisberger

525. Between 1967 and 2020, who was the youngest head coach to ever win a Super Bowl?

   a. Mike Tomlin

   b. John Harbaugh

   c. Sean McVay

   d. Sean Payton

526. Which players were involved in the play that resulted in the largest loss of yards on a single offensive snap in Super Bowl history?

527. Which team holds the record for the longest amount of time playing with a lead in the Super Bowl?

528. Which quarterback holds the record for the most passing yards in a Super Bowl game?

529. What team scored the lowest number of points in a Super Bowl victory?

530. Between 2010 and 2020, which Super Bowl became the most watched television broadcast of all time?

531. Who holds the record for the most Super Bowl wins by a player-turned-head coach, having won Super Bowls as both?

532. Kadarius Toney set a new Super Bowl record for the longest punt return in 2023. How long was the return?

533. Which team has played in four Super Bowls but never held a lead in the game?

DYNASTIES

534. Name the only franchise to win five Super Bowls before suffering a Super Bowl loss.

535. Despite their success, which franchise has allowed the same number of points they have scored in their five Super Bowl appearances?

536. Name the franchises that have had more Super Bowl–winning head coaches than Super Bowl–winning starting quarterbacks.

537. Only one Green Bay Packers quarterback has won the Super Bowl but was not named the game's MVP. Who is it?

538. The New York Giants have started four quarterbacks in the Super Bowl, and only one didn't win. Who was it?

539. Which franchise is the only one to win back-to-back Super Bowls with two different head coaches?

540. The Dallas Cowboys traded running back _____ to the Minnesota Vikings in exchange for multiple draft picks, which would be used to jump-start their dynasty.

541. Tom Brady won four Super Bowl MVPs while leading the New England Patriots to six titles. Which players won the other two Most Valuable Player awards?

542. Which two franchises have played each other a record three times in the Super Bowl?

543. Only one franchise has gone on to win two Super Bowls without playing a home playoff game at any time during those postseasons. Name the team.

544. Which franchise is the only one to win back-to-back Super Bowls twice in their history?

545. What franchise has seen three consecutive head coaches with at least one Super Bowl win?

546. Name the three New England Patriots quarterbacks to lose a Super Bowl.

547. Only two head coaches have gone at least three Super Bowl wins without a defeat. Who are they?

548. Which franchise holds the record for most points scored in a single Super Bowl between 1967 and 2020?

    a.   New England Patriots

    b.   San Francisco 49ers

    c.   Dallas Cowboys

    d.   Oakland Raiders

COMMERCIAL BREAKS

549. Which computer company gave Super Bowl viewers a commercial inspired by the novel *1984*?

550. Which restaurant chain gave Super Bowl viewers "The Showdown," featuring Larry Bird and Michael Jordan playing a game of Horse?

551. Which famous animals played football in a commercial in 1993, calling upon a zebra to be their replay official?

552. Which soft drink commercial featuring an injured Pittsburgh Steelers player and a young fan gained prominence when it aired during Super Bowl XIV (14)?

553. Super Bowl XXXII (32) saw which "Doritos Girl" become an overnight sensation after she starred in several commercials during the game?

554. What dot-com company created commercials so provocative that they could only air Super Bowl "teaser" ads directing viewers to their website to see the uncensored content?

555. Which first-round drafted quarterback was part of a controversial Super Bowl commercial months before he joined the NFL?

556. Which upstart fast food chain took a shot at their competitors in 1984 and gave Super Bowl viewers a catchphrase still used decades later?

557. Which Super Bowl VII (7) commercial featured a former Super Bowl MVP getting "creamed" by a future "Angel"?

558. Which online investment company "hired" a baby to advertise their company during Super Bowl XLII (42)?

559. When asked to make a choice during the 1980s Soda Wars, which "King of Pop" made the "Choice of a New Generation"?

560. The pairing of a Nike legend and a cartoon character set the stage for the first *Space Jam* movie when which advertisement aired during Super Bowl XXVI (26)?

561. Which candy bar manufacturer scored a touchdown when they hired Betty White for a Super Bowl XLIV (44) ad?

562. Which Super Bowl XLIX (49) car commercial used the famous "Handcuffed Lightning and Thrown Thunder in Jail" speech of Muhammad Ali to highlight an Olympic athlete, not their automobile.

563. During Super Bowl XXIX (29), a Budweiser commercial introduced three puppet frogs. What were the frogs' names?

564. What is the name of the now-defunct crypto company that featured a commercial with Larry David during Super Bowl LVII (57)

565. Which famous actor serenaded Jennifer Lopez as the singer of a fictional boy band in a Dunkin' Donuts commercial during Super Bowl LVIII (53)?

MVPS

566. Name the three players to wear No. 11 and win the Super Bowl MVP award from 1967 to 2020.

567. Name the first five players to win Super Bowl MVP honors while wearing No. 12.

568. From 1967 to 2020, what was the highest jersey number worn by a Super Bowl MVP?

   a. 80

   b. 81

   c. 95

   d. 99

569. Which two different players won Super Bowl MVPs in back-to-back years wearing No. 10?

570. Of the first seven running backs to have earned a Super Bowl MVP, who is the only one to have not reached the Hall of Fame before 2021?

571. Between 1967 and 2020, which two franchises saw a quarterback, running back, and wide receiver win Super Bowl MVP honors at least once?

572. Which two Super Bowl MVPs who won between 1967 and 2020 were born outside the United States?

573. Which San Francisco 49ers kicker might have been the first to receive a Super Bowl MVP snub?

   a. Ray Wersching

   b. Mike Cofer

   c. Doug Brien

   d. Robbie Gould

574. Who is the only NFL player to have won Super Bowl MVP while playing for the losing team?

575. Who was the first quarterback to win Super Bowl MVP without throwing a touchdown pass?

   a.   Bart Starr

   b.   Joe Namath

   c.   Terry Bradshaw

   d.   Jim Plunkett

576. True or False: Between 2000 and 2020 (up until Super Bowl XXXV (35)), no running back was named Super Bowl MVP.

577. Between 1967 and 2020, which two Super Bowl MVP quarterbacks threw for more than 400 yards?

578. True or False: Every wide receiver to win Super Bowl MVP had at least 100 yards and a touchdown in the game.

579. Who were the first NFL players to be named Co-MVPs of a Super Bowl?

580. Between 1967 and 2020, which franchise with multiple Super Bowl wins had never had a quarterback win the MVP?

581. How many different positions have won Super Bowl MVP?

582. In 2024, Patrick Mahomes became the fifth quarterback to win three Super Bowls. Which four other players have won three or more Super Bowls?

HALFTIME SHOWS

The evolution of the Super Bowl halftime show has in many ways mimicked that of the National Football League itself. In the early days of the AFL vs. NFL Championship Game, college marching bands entertained the fans, who had paid as little as $14 per ticket to watch the Super Bowl in person.

As the television audience and ticket prices continued to grow, bigger and bigger names in the music industry were added to the Super Bowl halftime show. With the arrival of musical legends like Michael Jackson, Diana Ross, and Beyoncé, the Super Bowl halftime show reached new heights, becoming almost as popular as the game itself, with some tuning in just to see the halftime performance, regardless of which teams were playing.

In many viewers' opinions, the Super Bowl XLI (41) halftime performance by Prince was one of the most electrifying and memorable. In the only Super Bowl that saw any significant rainfall, Prince performed his famous song "Purple Rain." When Prince was told it was raining before halftime, he said, "Good, let it rain more."

Other noteworthy acts over the years included the Rolling Stones, Bruce Springsteen, Madonna, Katy Perry, Lady Gaga, Jennifer Lopez, and Shakira.

Super Bowl halftime performers are not paid for their performances. However, the NFL does cover all production costs, and performers get the chance to reach a new audience by performing in front of the largest television audience each year. It is estimated that the 12- to 15-minute halftime show is worth about $24 to $30 million in exposure.

CHAPTER 6

BLOOPERS AND SURPRISES

In sports, the unexpected often provides a moment of humor and a lasting memory that becomes an unusual part of the game's history. For the NFL, these moments have come from commentators and fans as well as players and coaches, both on the field and in front of microphones. With such a long history and so much game footage, the NFL has never had a shortage of bloopers and surprises.

NFL WTF?

583. In a 2010 game between the Detroit Lions and Chicago Bears, what was the controversial call that involved Calvin Johnson?

584. During a snowy 1982 game between the New England Patriots and the Miami Dolphins, what was used to clear snow to give the Patriots a clear shot at kicking a game-winning field goal?

    a. Group of snow shovelers working for the Patriots

    b. Patriots players

    c. Snowplow

    d. Snowblower

585. In a 1998 overtime game between the Pittsburgh Steelers and the Detroit Lions, Jerome Bettis called _____ during the coin toss to start overtime, yet the referee thought he heard him say _____, which led to the Steelers losing the coin toss, and subsequently the game, since the Lions scored on their first possession of overtime.

586. In the 1999 "Catch 2" game between the San Francisco 49ers and the Green Bay Packers, which wrong call involved wide receiver Jerry Rice and helped the 49ers secure the win?

587. During the 2018 AFC Championship Game between the New England Patriots and the Kansas City Chiefs, which player was called offsides, which negated a Tom Brady interception?

588. In a 2014 NFC divisional playoff between the Dallas Cowboys and the Green Bay Packers, what was the controversial call that involved wide receiver Dez Bryant?

589. During the Music City Miracle between the Tennessee Titans and the Buffalo Bills, what should have been called on tight end Frank Wycheck on the Titans' final kickoff return—with 16 seconds remaining in the game—yet wasn't, due to inconclusive evidence?

590. During the 2009 NFC Championship Game between the New Orleans Saints and the Minnesota Vikings, what controversial call was missed and involved defensive end Bobby McCray?

591. During the 2001 AFC Divisional playoff game between the New England Patriots and the Oakland Raiders, what was the controversial call that involved Tom Brady?

592. During the 2002 NFC Wild Card game between the San Francisco 49ers and the New York Giants, what happened at the end of the game that was both highly controversial and potentially cost the Giants the game?

593. During a 2012 game between the Seattle Seahawks and the Green Bay Packers, what controversial call did the replacement referees make that determined the winner of the game?

a. Touchdown

b. Interception

c. Fumble

d. Incomplete Catch

594. During a 1989 game between the San Francisco 49ers and New Orleans Saints, what controversial moment did the referees miss that involved wide receiver Jerry Rice and his 60-yard touchdown?

595. During a 1998 game between the New York Jets and the Seattle Seahawks, Jets quarterback Vinny Testaverde dove for the game-winning touchdown. After the game, the referee realized the touchdown was the wrong call, because he mistook which item for the football as it crossed the goal line?

a. Glove

b. Mouthpiece

c. Hair

d. Helmet

596. During a 1989 game between the San Francisco 49ers and the New Orleans Saints, what controversial moment involved 49ers wide receiver John Taylor?

597. During a 2001 game between the Jacksonville Jaguars and the Cleveland Browns, what controversial moment happened that cost the Browns the game?

598. During a 2008 game between the Denver Broncos and the San Diego Chargers, what controversial moment involved referee Ed Hochuli and played a role in the Broncos winning?

    a.   Hochuli blew a play dead after the Broncos fumbled the ball

    b.   Hochuli awarded the Broncos an extra challenge

    c.   Hochuli blocked a player during a critical play

    d.   Hochuli called a false touchdown

599. Which Super Bowl is well known for having multiple controversial calls, to the point that referee Bill Leavy admitted that the calls had a bearing on the outcome of the game?

600. During the 1979 AFC Championship Game between the Pittsburgh Steelers and the Houston Oilers, which player was ruled out of bounds on a touchdown, in a call that is now viewed as one of the worst in NFL history?

601. What controversial call was missed in the 2018 NFC Championship Game between the New Orleans Saints and the Los Angeles Rams?

602. During a 1997 game between the New York Jets and the Detroit Lions, what controversial moment happened that cost the Jets the game?

603. During a Wild Card game between the Cincinnati Bengals and the Pittsburgh Steelers, Bengals cornerback Adam "Pacman" Jones was called for an _____ that involved Steelers outside linebackers coach Joey Porter, which put the Steelers in position to kick the game-winning field goal.

604. During the original Hail Mary play, which involved the Dallas Cowboys and the Minnesota Vikings, what call was missed by referees that involved wide receiver Drew Pearson?

605. During the 2012 NFC Championship Game between the Atlanta Falcons and the San Francisco 49ers, what was the controversial moment that involved wide receiver Roddy White and linebacker NaVorro Bowman?

606. During Super Bowl L (50), between the Denver Broncos and the Carolina Panthers, what was the controversial moment that involved Panthers wide receiver Jerricho Cotchery?

607. During the Super Bowl XLIII (43) game between the Pittsburgh Steelers and the Arizona Cardinals, what play still has fans questioning years later if it was the correct call?

608. Which team lost two draft picks and had its coach suspended and fined $1.5 million after being found guilty of tampering with Tom Brady and Sean Payton?

609. Who was the first player to ever wear Number 0 in NFL history?

FANS GONE WILD

610. In a 2005 game between the Green Bay Packers and the Cincinnati Bengals, a fan ran onto the field and took the football from which player?

611. In a 2008 game between the New England Patriots and the Arizona Cardinals, which Patriots linebacker was tackled by a fan who ran onto the field?

612. In the 2018 AFC Championship Game between the New England Patriots and the Kansas City Chiefs, a fan used a laser pointer from the stands to distract which player?

613. In a 1985 game between the San Francisco 49ers and the Denver Broncos, what was thrown at the field goal holder that distracted him enough to mishandle the snap?

614. In a 2011 game between the Chicago Bears and the Tampa Bay Buccaneers, a fan ran onto the field attempting to high-five players. Which Bears player did the fan successfully high-five?

615. In a 2005 Christmas Eve game between the Pittsburgh Steelers and the Cleveland Browns, which Steelers player body slammed a fan to the ground after the fan ran onto the field?

616. In a 2018 regular season game between the New England Patriots and the Kansas City Chiefs, which player had a beer thrown in his face by a fan after scoring a touchdown?

617. In a 2008 game between the New York Jets and the Seattle Seahawks, which Jets player was fined for picking up a large pile of snow and throwing it at a fan after the game?

618. In a 1999 game between the Oakland Raiders and the Denver Broncos, which Raiders player punched a fan after getting hit in the face with a snowball?

619. During the 2017 NFL Pro Bowl, which running back assisted stadium security in stopping a fan who ran onto the field?

620. During Super Bowl XXXVIII (38), between the New England Patriots and the Carolina Panthers, which Patriots player hit a fan who was streaking on the field?

621. During a 2015 AFC Wild Card playoff game between the Pittsburgh Steelers and the Cincinnati Bengals, fans in the stands threw trash at a player as he was carted to the locker room. Which player was trash thrown at?

622. During a 1999 game between the Philadelphia Eagles and the Dallas Cowboys, Eagles fans cheered when a Cowboys player lay motionless on the field after sustaining an injury. Which Cowboys player was it?

623. During a 1989 game between the Denver Broncos and the Cleveland Browns, which Broncos player was pelted with Milk-Bone dog treats and batteries by Browns fans?

624. During a 2007 game between the Dallas Cowboys and the Green Bay Packers, which Cowboys player grabbed a fan's popcorn and dumped it into his own face mask after scoring a touchdown?

625. Against which team did New York Giants fans begin throwing snowballs in 1995, injuring their 60-year-old equipment manager?

MUSICAL MEMORIES

626. The _____ was a rap song performed by the 1985 Chicago Bears.

627. The "LT Slide Electric Glide," noted for being highly similar to the "Cha-Cha Slide," was which player's musical release?

628. True or False: Quarterback and commentator Terry Bradshaw created an album that had a single on the Billboard Hot 100.

629. Name the three Dallas Cowboys offensive linemen that make up the heavy metal band Free Reign, which they formed in 2007.

630. Deion Sanders performed his single _____ when he appeared on *Saturday Night Live in* 1995 as the host and musical guest.

631. Which Dallas Cowboys quarterback created a country album called *Country Cowboy*?

632. Former New Orleans Saints offensive lineman Kyle Turley created which song that talks about the rise and fall of NFL players?

633. What is the name of the only song released by Cincinnati Bengals cornerback Adam "Pacman" Jones?

634. Which former All-Pro Pittsburgh Steelers running back released a song called "Target," which discussed his contract dispute with the team?

635. Which former Dallas Cowboys wide receiver released a song called "80 Stings," which mentions Dak Prescott and Jerry Jones?

BLOOPERS AND FLUBS

636. Which former Philadelphia Eagles receiver started celebrating a touchdown prematurely and let the football drop out of his hands before crossing the goal line?

637. Which NFL quarterback formed a "W" with his fingers and pretended to eat it during a pregame speech to pump up his teammates, only for his team to end up losing the game?

638. Which NFL quarterback mishandled a game-winning field goal snap during the 2006 playoffs, which ended up costing his team a win?

639. Which NFL quarterback ran out of the back of the end zone during a play, yet had no clue during the play that he had just committed a safety?

640. Which Tennessee Titans kick returner received a kickoff with one foot out of the end zone and one foot in, and decided to kneel in the end zone instead of advancing the football, which resulted in a safety?

641. Which Houston Texans quarterback tried to remake the famous "John Elway helicopter leap" to pick up a first down and secure the win, yet ended up fumbling, and cost his team the game by allowing the other team to return the dropped ball for a touchdown?

642. Which NFL quarterback was sacked for 30 yards against the Miami Dolphins during a scramble to try to find an open receiver?

643. Which NFL quarterback held up four fingers to signal to the referees that it was fourth down, yet the quarterback didn't realize he had just played a fourth down?

644. Which NFL wide receiver punched a kicking net out of frustration, then was hit in the face when the kicking net swung back down?

645. In a Thanksgiving Day game between the Dallas Cowboys and the Miami Dolphins, which Cowboys player mistakenly touched a blocked field goal ball, which was then recovered by Miami, thus giving Miami a second chance at a field goal—which ended up winning the game?

646. In a 1964 NFL game between the Minnesota Vikings and the San Francisco 49ers, which Vikings player recovered a fumble and ran to the wrong end zone and proceeded to celebrate and throw the football out of bounds, resulting in a safety?

647. In a 2002 NFL game between the Kansas City Chiefs and the Cleveland Browns, which Browns player threw their helmet in celebration with seconds left, thinking the game was over, and ultimately got called for an unsportsmanlike conduct penalty that pushed the Chiefs into field goal range to win the game.

648. Name the Minnesota Vikings kicker who missed a 38-yard field goal attempt in the 1998 NFC Championship Game against the Atlanta Falcons that would have secured a trip to the Super Bowl for the Vikings?

649. Name the Washington Commanders coach who made the mistake of calling back-to-back timeouts in a 2007 game against the Buffalo Bills, with the hope of "icing" the opposing Bills kicker to miss the 51-yard game-winning field goal. Yet, calling back-to-back timeouts resulted in a 15-yard unsportsmanlike conduct penalty and resulted in an easy field goal attempt for the Bills, which the Bills made.

650. Name the New Orleans Saints quarterback who threw the ball 25 yards backward in a 2004 game against the San Diego Chargers.

651. Name the former Raiders quarterback who lied to his team by saying he watched film, yet the team knew he didn't since they gave him blank film tapes as a test to see if he was truly studying.

652. True or False: In a 2020 game between the New York Giants and the Philadelphia Eagles, Giants quarterback Daniel Jones tripped on a potential 88-yard touchdown when there was no defender close to potentially stop him from scoring.

653. In Super Bowl XXVI (26) between the Buffalo Bills and Washington Commanders, this Buffalo Bills player lost his helmet and missed the first two plays of the game looking for it.

654. Name the Detroit Lions player who tore his ACL during a sack celebration of Aaron Rodgers in a 2014 game against the Green Bay Packers.

655. Name the Washington Commanders quarterback who injured himself in a 1997 game against the New York Giants by head-butting a wall after scoring a touchdown.

656. In 1964, who was the Minnesota Vikings defensive end that picked up a fumble and ran 66 yards the wrong way into his own end zone?

WHO SAID IT? COMMENTATOR EDITION

657. Which NFL commentator famously said, "That is a disgusting act by Randy Moss," after Moss mooned Green Bay Packers fans?

658. Which NFL commentator gave a play-by-play of a fan running onto the field, saying, "Hey, somebody has run out on the field. Some goofball in a hat and a red shirt. Now he takes off the shirt! He's running down the middle by the 50, he's at the 30! He's bare-chested and banging his chest. Now he runs the opposite way. He runs to the 50! He runs to the 40! The guy is drunk, but there he goes"?

659. Which NFL commentator famously yelled through an entire play-by-play call by saying, "Oh, caught! Stokley! Down the sideline! Can he catch him!? Stokley! Wow"?

660. Which NFL commentator said, "He's a Popeyes biscuit away from being a tight end" when referring to Kelvin Benjamin?

661. Which NFL commentator said, "[Lamar] Jackson takes it himself, look at him dart back and forth–" Oh! He broke his ankles! Now he's got an entourage! And he's got a touchdown! He is Houdini!"?

662. Which NFL commentator said, "The winner of this game is going to be whoever has the most points on the scoreboard at the end of the game"?

663. Which former NFL quarterback-turned-commentator said, "It's ridiculous to think that you get to play a game you love for a job you get paid for"?

664. Which NFL commentator famously said, "Unicorns! Show ponies! Where's the beef?!" after watching New England Patriots quarterback Tom Brady complete a game-winning drive against the New Orleans Saints in 2013?

665. Which NFL commentator said, "At least he held on to his helmet," in reference to Jamaal Charles fumbling the ball, which would help seal the win for the Denver Broncos over the Kansas City Chiefs in 2015?

666. Which NFL Commentator said, "A high ankle sprain is generally higher up on the ankle"?

THE USFL

One of those memorable periods in the history of professional football was from 1983 to 1985, when the United States Football League, or USFL, tried to compete with the National Football League. The USFL stole players from the NFL by offering bigger contracts and the promise of being part of something bigger: a chance to topple the monopoly of the NFL.

The upstart USFL signed 1982 Heisman Trophy winner Herschel Walker out of Georgia before the 1983 NFL Draft, providing a level of credibility to the league before it ever played a game. Walker signed with the New Jersey Generals, and the running back was joined by Heisman quarterback Doug Flutie, who was paid $7 million by the team in 1985. That contract, at the time, made the Boston College alum the highest-paid player in pro football history, and, at least for one season, kept the 1984 Heisman Trophy winner away from the NFL.

Facing a lack of fan support and poor television ratings, the USFL suspended operations before the 1986 season and would never take the field again, which led to USFL players, including Herschel Walker and Doug Flutie, going to the NFL and having long careers. A last-ditch effort saw the league file an antitrust lawsuit against the NFL. The failed league did, on paper, win their case, but the $1 in damages awarded by the court (which was tripled to $3 under antitrust laws) saw the league fade into the history books.

The USFL did return in 2022, and in 2023, the USFL and the XFL announced they would be merging into the United Football League starting in 2024.

CHAPTER 7

HALL OF FAME

Over 23,000 players, joined by their coaches and executives, have been a part of the NFL, but less than 400 have been elected to the Pro Football Hall of Fame since it opened in 1963. Their names comprise a select group of pioneers and superstars who have helped shape the National Football League since its birth in 1920.

While football is considered by many to be the ultimate team game, being enshrined into the Pro Football Hall of Fame is the ultimate individual achievement for any player. This achievement requires something a little extra special from the player to go along with their stats and awards: the precision route running of Jerry Rice or the pinpoint accuracy of Joe Montana. The sheer will and determination of Walter Payton or the ankle-breaking abilities of Barry Sanders. Those are the kinds of abilities that not only make highlights, but make Hall of Fame players, with all those who come after them still trying to top those who came before.

Receiving the now-iconic gold jacket for the Pro Football Hall of Fame signifies that person was indeed the "gold standard" in the NFL.

PLAYERS

667. Who are the four Hall of Fame players who began their NFL careers in the USFL?

668. This Cincinnati Bengals player is the only Hall of Famer to have played all of his games for Cincinnati.

669. Perhaps one of the most decorated players in football history, which running back is the only player to win the Heisman Trophy and a national championship in college, and then an NFL MVP award, a Super Bowl, and a Super Bowl MVP award?

670. Only three exclusive punters/placekickers are in the Hall of Fame. Who are they?

671. Which player won the Heisman Trophy, was drafted first over-all, won two Super Bowl titles, and was awarded Super Bowl MVP, but is *not* in the Hall of Fame?

672. In 2021, which cornerback became the fifth Hall of Famer with a Heisman Trophy (University of Michigan) and a Super Bowl (Green Bay Packers)?

673. Which wide receiver holds the record for the number of times he was a Hall of Fame finalist before finally getting enshrined?

674. Name the first Heisman Trophy–winning quarterback to be enshrined in the Pro Football Hall of Fame.

675. Which player was the first to enter the Hall of Fame as a Super Bowl winner?

676. It only took which running back 13 years to add a Heisman Trophy and a gold Hall of Fame jacket to his football legacy?

677. There are only three quarterbacks to have started their careers during the Super Bowl era (starting in 1967) and made the Hall of Fame without winning a Super Bowl. Who are they?

678. Which wide receiver entered the Hall of Fame with the fewest receiving yards in the Super Bowl era?

679. Which Hall of Famer is the great-great-great-grandson of the founder of Brigham Young University, which is also the player's alma mater?

680. Between 1967 and 2020, which running back had the fewest career rushing yards among Hall of Famers?

   a.   John Riggins

   b.   Floyd Little

   c.   Franco Harris

   d.   Terrell Davis

681. Between 1967 and 2020, which quarterback had the fewest career passing yards among Hall of Famers?

   a.   Ken Stabler

   b.   Bob Griese

   c.   Troy Aikman

   d.   Roger Staubach

682. Name the first defensive player in the Hall of Fame to have entered the NFL as an undrafted free agent.

683. Which quarterback is the only quarterback in the Hall of Fame who entered the NFL as an undrafted free agent?

684. Name the two NFL players who were strictly kickers and are currently in the Hall of Fame?

685. Name all the Hall of Fame quarterbacks who attended one of the following three universities: Florida State University, Ohio State University, and the University of Southern California.

686. Name the first player to be inducted into the Hall of Fame with 14 Pro Bowl selections in his career.

687. Name the first player to be inducted in to both the Pro Football Hall of Fame and the Arena Football Hall of Fame.

688. Name the Hall of Fame quarterback whose son won Super Bowl XXXIII (33) for the Denver Broncos.

689. Name the Hall of Fame player who led the NFL Players Association strike the same year he was enshrined.

690. Name the first two Pro Football Hall of Famers who also played Major League Baseball.

691. Name the first person enshrined in both the Pro Football Hall of Fame and National Baseball Hall of Fame.

692. Which Hall of Fame kicker was born outside of the United States and even mentioned his birth country in the first few sentences of his Hall of Fame speech?

693. Which Hall of Fame quarterback formed one of the most well-known quarterback-center pairs in NFL history with Hall of Fame center Mike Webster?

694. This legendary quarterback ended his career and went into the Hall of Fame with the most interceptions thrown in NFL history at the time.

695. This Hall of Fame quarterback went undrafted in the 1994 NFL draft and ended up stocking shelves at a Hy-Vee grocery store before getting another opportunity to play football.

696. This Hall of Fame quarterback was the first quarterback to pass for 4,000 yards in a season.

697. Who was the first Jacksonville Jaguars player enshrined in the Pro Football Hall of Fame in 2022?

698. Which Pro Football Hall of Fame member was inducted without playing a single game in the NFL?

699. This Hall of Fame member was the centerpiece of the New York Sack Exchange, the fearsome defensive line of the New York Jets.

COACHES

700. Name the first Hall of Famer who was a head coach, owner, and commissioner.

701. There are three Hall of Fame head coaches with four Super Bowl losses apiece. Name them.

702. Which four head coaches worked for both AFL and NFL teams during their Hall of Fame careers?

703. Name the first Super Bowl–winning head coach to be enshrined in the Hall of Fame.

704. True or False: San Francisco 49ers Hall of Fame head coach Bill Walsh had multiple assistant coaches become head coaches and led their teams to Super Bowl wins.

705. _____ was the only head coach with at least 200 career wins who was not in the Hall of Fame after the 2023 season.

706. Only one Super Bowl–era head coach has made the Hall of Fame after working for four difference franchises. Who is that head coach?

707. Rank these five Hall of Fame head coaches by the number of wins they had during their NFL careers:

   a. Tom Flores

   b. Jimmy Johnson

   c. Vince Lombardi

   d. John Madden

   e. Bill Walsh

708. Which two Super Bowl–winning head coaches have the most career victories without being enshrined in the Hall of Fame?

709. Name the only Hall of Fame head coach who has an NFL stadium named after them.

710. Which "head coach" had a 12–33 win/loss record but was still inducted into the Hall of Fame?

711. Which franchise did Hall of Fame head coach John Madden, also known for his popular video game, lead for 10 seasons before turning to a broadcasting career?

712. Despite never reaching the Super Bowl, which head coach employed four future Super Bowl–winning head coaches during his career, two of which are in the Hall of Fame?

713. Which Super Bowl matchup saw both head coaches voted into the Hall of Fame as players and not coaches?

714. Which head coach coached for four seasons after being inducted into the Hall of Fame?

715. In the Super Bowl era, which Hall of Famer has the best win percentage among head coaches who have never won a Super Bowl?

716. The name of Hall of Fame head coach Vince Lombardi is on the trophy given to the Super Bowl winner, but that hasn't always been the case. Which Super Bowl was the first to give a "Lombardi Trophy" to its winner?

717. Which head coach was the first to win the Super Bowl with a Wild Card team?

718. Hall of Fame head coach John Madden had an extreme fear of what?

719. This Super Bowl–winning head coach attended the same Big Ten school his Super Bowl MVP–winning quarterback did. What school did both the head coach and quarterback attend?

720. Which head coach was the first enshrined in the Hall of Fame with both a college national championship and a Super Bowl championship during their career?

721. Name the only two head coaches to make playoff appearances in each of their first six seasons as head coaches in the NFL and to make the Hall of Fame.

722. Six-time Super Bowl winner Bill Belichick called which head coach "The greatest coach in the history of professional football, clear and simple"?

723. Who was the first Black head coach enshrined in the Pro Football Hall of Fame?

724. Which NFL coach is the only individual to have been inducted into both the Pro Football Hall of Fame and College Football Hall of Fame as a coach?

OWNERS & EXECUTIVES

725. The name of which AFL cofounder and franchise owner is on the trophy given to the winner of the AFC Championship Game?

726. The name of which NFL cofounder, franchise owner, and longtime head coach is on the trophy given to the winner of the NFC Championship Game?

727. Which Hall of Fame NFL owner opened up the West Coast to major sports by moving the Rams to Los Angeles?

728. This franchise has a father and son in the Hall of Fame as owners, with the third generation of the same family currently running the family franchise.

729. Name the only NFL owner to have their team make four straight Super Bowl appearances.

730. What longtime Hall of Fame general manager guided teams to five Super Bowl appearances, only to win one, and sat players on a 14–0 team, forgoing a chance at a perfect season.

731. Which Hall of Fame father-and-son duo helped build the NFL not with their arms or legs, but with their cameras?

732. What owner went from winning Super Bowls at a record-setting pace to facing legal issues, giving up control of his franchise, and then receiving a presidential pardon?

733. Which Hall of Fame general manager won a Super Bowl with 27 free agents on the team's roster?

734. Which general manager drafted quarterback Ken Stabler and traded for quarterback Brett Favre during his Hall of Fame career?

735. Which franchise saw its founder and its best-known head coach both end their storied Hall of Fame careers after working for the Washington Commanders?

736. Which Hall of Famer said his biggest regret was how the November 24, 1963, schedule was handled?

737. Which Hall of Fame executive was hired by the New York Giants at the recommendation of then-commissioner Pete Rozelle?

738. Which Hall of Fame general manager was the president and CEO of the short-lived World League of American Football in 1989 and 1990?

739. Which person was given the honor of informing everyone that they have been selected to become a Pro Football Hall of Famer until his retirement in 2021?

WHO SAID IT?

740. What running back said at the end of their enshrinement speech, "You've got to have the ability and understand that you're going to fail. But it's how you recover that makes you a better person"?

741. Which Dallas Cowboys legend told the crowd during their Hall of Fame speech, "Look up, get up, and don't ever give up"?

742. Which quarterback said, while giving their 1989 induction speech, "What I wouldn't give right now to put my hands under Mike Webster's butt just one more time"?

743. Which quarterback ironically said, during their 2016 speech, "I have never thrown an interception that has been my fault, according to my mother-in-law, Ann"?

744. Which player paid homage to his hometown of Rand, West Virginia in 2018 by saying, "All y'all West Virginians want to see this gold jacket? Meet me at the town center tomorrow at 4:30"?

745. Which Hall of Famer said during his 2000 induction speech, "In my opinion, baseball is America's pastime, but football is truly America's passion"?

746. Who is the linebacker that stated, during his Hall of Fame induction speech in 1990, "If I could start my life all over again, I would be a professional football player. And you damn well better believe I'd be a Pittsburgh Steeler"?

747. Which Hall of Famer said during his Hall of Fame induction speech, "There are no more routes to run, no more touchdowns to score, no more records to set. That young boy from Mississippi has finally stopped running. Let me stand here and catch my breath. Let me inhale it all in one more time"?

748. Which Hall of Fame wide receiver said during his induction, "This game gave me identity. It gave me a sense of purpose"?

749. Which quarterback hilariously said during his Hall of Fame induction speech, "I want to give a special thanks to my old rival, Ray Lewis, for being here tonight. Ray just finished giving his speech that he started in 2018"?

750. Which Hall of Fame quarterback said, "The road to our dreams often has detours. Sometimes you gotta do what you gotta do while you're waiting to do what you were born to do. Thus, my infamous stint at the grocery store."

HALL OF FAME TIMELINE

You may wonder why the Pro Football Hall of Fame is in Canton, Ohio, home of zero NFL teams. Interestingly, the city lobbied for it, leading a December 1959 newspaper headline—"PRO FOOTBALL NEEDS A HALL OF FAME AND LOGICAL SITE IS HERE"—into a groundbreaking ceremony in August 1962 and then into the Hall's first enshrinement ceremony, in September 1963.

From the first class, which included George Halas, Earl "Curly" Lambeau, and Jim Thorpe, to each new class, the history of professional football is etched in stone. As the Hall itself grew, so too did the enshrinement ceremony itself, becoming a special moment for fans to attend or watch on television every summer.

Canton has seen its fair share of football history. New York Giants safety Emlen Tunnell became the first player of color inducted, in 1967. Tunnell, who once said, "I could make tackles until I'm 50. Your body may go, but your heart doesn't," was a great player deserving of any and all accolades. In 2005, Tunnell was joined in the Hall of Fame by "Fritz" Pollard, the first Black player/coach in league history. Quarterback Len Dawson became the first Canton native enshrined, and in 1999, the Cleveland Browns marked their return to the NFL by playing in the Hall of Fame Game.

It wasn't until 2002 that the Hall held its enshrinement ceremony in Hall of Fame Stadium—before that, they hosted the event on the steps of the Hall itself. One Hall of Famer, Terrell Owens, did not attend his own induction ceremony in 2018 in protest of the two-year wait he had after becoming eligible to be named a Hall of Fame player. It wasn't until 2019 that Owens unveiled his bronze bust and received his iconic gold jacket, which has been a symbol of being in the Pro Football Hall of Fame since its debut in 1978.

ANSWER KEY

CHAPTER 1
THE DRAFT

GENERAL

1. Quarterbacks Charlie Ward from Florida State University in 1993 and Jason White from the University of Oklahoma in 2003.

2. Terry Bradshaw in 1970 by the Pittsburgh Steelers, John Elway in 1983 by the Denver Broncos, and Troy Aikman in 1989 by the Dallas Cowboys.

3. University of Miami quarterback Craig Erickson was drafted by the Philadelphia Eagles in 1991 and the Tampa Bay Buccaneers in 1992.

4. D. Ki-Jana Carter. The Penn State running back was drafted first overall in 1995 by the Cincinnati Bengals.

5. Buck Buchanan was drafted by the Kansas City Chiefs in 1963, and the Grambling State defensive tackle was inducted into the Hall of Fame in 1996.

6. The Houston Oilers' Earl Campbell in 1978, the Detroit Lions' Billy Sims in 1980, and the New Orleans Saints' George Rogers in 1981.

7. The St. Louis Rams' Sam Bradford in 2010, the Carolina Panthers' Cam Newton in 2011, and the Arizona Cardinals' Kyler Murray in 2019.

8. The Baltimore Ravens, Denver Broncos, and Seattle Seahawks.

9. Archie Manning was drafted second overall by the New Orleans Saints in 1971.

10. Oklahoma, Notre Dame, and Southern California have each had five players taken first overall.

11. The Detroit Lions drafted running back Barry Sanders in 1988 and quarterback Andre Ward in 1989. The Tennessee Titans drafted quarterback Marcus Mariota and running back Derrick Henry in 2014 and 2015, respectively.

12. Gary Kubiak was drafted by the Denver Broncos in 1983 out of Texas A&M, and he later became the head coach for the Houston Texans and the Denver Broncos.

13. C. Keyshawn Johnson was taken first overall by the New York Jets in the 1996 Draft.

14. Sebastian Janikowski was selected 17th overall by the Oakland Raiders in the 2000 Draft.

15. Defensive end Bruce Smith (first overall by the Buffalo Bills), defensive end Chris Doleman (fourth overall by the Minnesota Vikings), wide receiver Jerry Rice (16th overall by the San Francisco 49ers), wide receiver Andre Reed (fourth round by the Buffalo Bills), line backer Kevin Greene (fifth round by the St. Louis Rams).

16. Lawrence Taylor (second overall by the New York Giants), Kenny Easley (fourth overall by the Seattle Seahawks), Ronnie Lott (eighth overall by the San Francisco 49ers), Mike Singletary (38th overall by the Chicago Bears), Howie Long (48th overall by the Oakland Raiders), and Rickey Jackson (51st overall by the New Orleans Saints).

17. Steve Spurrier won the 1966 Heisman Trophy and was the Washington Commanders head coach in 2002 and 2003.

18. David Carr (2002) and Eli Manning (2004) were teammates on the New York Giants' winning team for Super Bowl XLVI (46). Manning also won Super Bowl XLII (42) with the Giants.

19. Eric Fisher was drafted first overall by the Kansas City Chiefs in 2013 and won Super Bowl LIV (54) with them.

20. Dan McGwire (San Diego State) was selected 16th by the Seattle Seahawks and Todd Marinovich (USC) was taken 24th by the Oakland Raiders in 1991. Brett Favre went 33rd overall to the Atlanta Falcons before being traded to the Green Bay Packers.

21. The SEC.

22. Strength of schedule.

23. 1980.

AFC EAST

24. In 1969, the Buffalo Bills drafted O.J. Simpson first overall, and in 1985 they selected Bruce Smith.

25. False. The Miami Dolphins selected DE Jason Taylor in the third round of the 1997 Draft, and he made the Hall of Fame in 2017.

26. Gronkowski was the 42nd pick in the 2010 Draft, Edelman was the 232nd pick in 2009, Brady was the 199th pick in 2000, Vinatieri went undrafted in 1996, and Brown was the 198th pick in 1993.

27. Greg McElroy (2011), Geno Smith (2013), Tajh Boyd (2014), Bryce Petty (2015), Christian Hackenberg (2016), Sam Darnold (2018), James Morgan (2020), Zach Wilson (2021).

28. Kliff Kingsbury was drafted 201st in 2003 by the New England Patriots and began the 2021 season as the Arizona Cardinal's head coach.

29. In 2008, the Dolphins selected offensive tackle Jake Long with the first overall pick, the only time in franchise history that they made the first pick in any draft.

30. False. The Jets drafted running back John Riggins, a member of the Hall of Fame Class of 1992, in 1971.

31. The Bills selected Frank Reich out of Maryland in the third round of the 1985 Draft.

32. University of Michigan defensive back Ty Law and University of Pittsburgh running back Curtis Martin were both drafted by New England in 1995.

33. Quarterback Josh Allen joined defensive tackle Pat Rabold (1989) and defensive back John Wendling (2007) as the third player drafted by the Buffalo Bills from the University of Wyoming.

AFC NORTH

34. Three: offensive tackle Jonathan Ogden, linebacker Ray Lewis, and defensive back Ed Reed.

35. In 1936, the Steelers drafted Notre Dame running back William Shakespeare.

36. D. Ken Anderson, who is the Cincinnati Bengals' all-time passing leader with 32,838 passing yards.

37. True. The last player drafted by Cleveland to make the Hall of Fame was Ozzie Newsome. The Alabama tight end was selected in the first round in 1978.

38. University of Georgia quarterback Eric Zeier was a third-round pick of the Browns in 1995.

39. Chad Johnson and T.J. Houshmandzadeh were both drafted in 2001 out of Oregon State.

40. Defensive tackle Joe Greene was drafted in 1969, quarterback Terry Bradshaw and cornerback Mel Blount in 1970, outside linebacker Jack Ham in 1971, and running back Franco Harris in 1972.

41. Quarterback Joe Flacco (2008) and center Gino Gradkowski (2012) both played for the Delaware Blue Hens and were on the Ravens team that won Super Bowl XLVII (47).

42. Wide receiver Plaxico Burress was a first-round pick in 2000, running back Le'Veon Bell was a second-round pick in 2013, and cornerback Justin Layne was a third-round pick in 2019.

43. Hines Ward has 1,000 career catches, the most of anyone drafted in 1998 and the most in Pittsburgh Steelers' history. Hall of Famer Randy Moss had 982 career receptions.

AFC SOUTH

44. Running back Marshall Faulk (1994), wide receiver Marvin Harrison (1996), quarterback Peyton Manning (1998), and running back Edgerrin James (1999).

45. Tight end Owen Daniels (2006) and defensive end J.J. Watt (2011).

46. Linebacker Andre Branch was drafted by the Jacksonville Jaguars in 2012 out of Clemson University.

47. Eddie George was the last first-round pick of the Houston Oilers in 1996.

48. Wide receiver Kevin Dyson was the first offensive player taken in the first round by the Titans after they moved to Tennessee. Quarterback Vince Young was the second offensive player taken in the first round.

49. John Elway was drafted by the Baltimore Colts in 1983. Peyton Manning was drafted by the Indianapolis Colts in 1998.

50. USC quarterback Rob Johnson was taken in the fourth round of the Jacksonville Jaguars' first draft in 1995.

51. The Indianapolis Colts drafted linebacker Quentin Coryatt in 1992 and Trev Alberts in 1994.

52. Cornerback Dunta Robinson (2004), cornerback Fred Bennett (2007), strong safety D.J. Swearinger (2013), and defensive end Jadeveon Clowney (2014).

53. Randy Bullock, out of Texas A&M, was drafted by the Texans in the 2012 Draft.

AFC WEST

54. Hall of Famer Ken Stabler (1968), David Humm (1975), and Todd Marinovich (1990).

55. Todd Blackledge in 1983.

56. Ohio State running back Maurice Clarett was drafted by the Denver Broncos in 2005 and never played a game in the NFL.

57. Hall of Fame running back LaDainian Tomlinson (first round) and quarterback Drew Brees (second round) were the first two players selected by the Chargers in 2001.

58. False. New Orleans' Michael Thomas entered 2021 with more receptions and receiving yardage than Kansas City's Tyreek Hill, who was second in both categories.

59. The Raiders drafted punter Ray Guy with the 23rd overall pick in the 1973 Draft. Through 2023, Guy was the only punter in the Pro Football Hall of Fame.

60. Terrell Davis was drafted in the sixth round in 1995, and only Davis and Curtis Martin made the Hall of Fame as a running back out of that year's class.

61. In 1979, the Chargers drafted future Hall of Fame tight end Kellen Winslow.

62. Defensive tackle Darrell Russell (1997), quarterback Todd Marinovich (1991), center Don Mosebar (1983), and running back Marcus Allen (1982).

63. Sylvester Morris (2000), Dwayne Bowe (2007), Jonathan Baldwin (2011), and Mecole Hardman (2019).

NFC EAST

64. Round 2. Brian Dawkins was drafted in Round 2 with the 61st overall pick during the 1996 NFL Draft.

65. B. The fourth overall pick was used to select defensive end Reggie White.

66. False. Donovan McNabb was drafted in the first round, second overall, in the 1999 NFL Draft.

67. Lawrence Taylor was drafted second overall, after running back George Rogers, in the 1981 NFL Draft.

68. True.

69. C. Art Monk was drafted in the first round, 18th overall, of the 1980 NFL Draft.

70. Darrell Green was drafted in the first round, 28th overall, of the 1983 NFL Draft.

71. Troy Aikman was drafted by the Dallas Cowboys with the first overall pick of the 1989 NFL Draft.

72. Michael Irvin, who was drafted in the first round, was the 11th overall pick of the 1988 NFL Draft.

73. Tony Dorsett.

NFC NORTH

74. Ed "Too Tall" Jones.

75. False: Walter Payton was drafted fourth overall in the 1975 NFL Draft.

76. A. Brian Urlacher was drafted by the Chicago Bears in the first round, ninth overall, of the 2000 NFL Draft.

77. Donald Driver was drafted by the Green Bay Packers in the seventh round, 213th overall, of the 1999 NFL Draft.

78. D. Aaron Rodgers was drafted with the 24th overall pick by the Green Bay Packers.

79. Javon Walker, who was drafted in the first round, 20th overall, of the 2002 NFL Draft.

80. Calvin Johnson, who was drafted in the first round, second overall, of the 2007 NFL Draft.

81. C. Barry Sanders was drafted third overall in the 1989 NFL Draft.

82. False. Ndamukong Suh was drafted second overall in the 2010 NFL Draft.

83. Wide receivers Randy Moss and Percy Harvin.

84. D. Adrian Peterson was drafted with the seventh overall pick in the 2007 NFL Draft.

NFC SOUTH

85. Running back Deuce McAllister, who was drafted in the first round, 23rd overall, of the 2001 NFL Draft.

86. True.

87. Ricky Williams.

88. Quarterback Cam Newton (Offensive Rookie of the Year) in the 2011 Draft and linebacker Luke Kuechly (Defensive Rookie of the Year) in 2012.

89. False. Wide receiver Steve Smith Sr. was drafted by the Carolina Panthers in the third round, 74th overall, of the 2001 NFL Draft.

90. Quarterback Michael Vick, who was the first overall pick of the 2001 NFL Draft.

91. Michael Jenkins in 2004 and Roddy White in 2005.

92. Defensive tackle Warren Sapp and linebacker Derrick Brooks in 1995.

93. Bo Jackson, who was drafted first overall in the 1986 NFL Draft.

94. The 2002 and 2003 first-round draft picks were used by the Tampa Bay Buccaneers to acquire Jon Gruden.

NFC WEST

95. C. Richard Sherman was drafted by the Seattle Seahawks in the fifth round, 154th overall.

96. The first- and third-round picks in 2001.

97. True.

98. Jerome Bettis, who was drafted in the first round, 10th overall, by the Los Angeles Rams in the 1993 NFL Draft.

99. Quarterbacks Jared Goff in 2016 and Sam Bradford in 2010.

100. A. Larry Fitzgerald was drafted in the first round, third overall, in the 2004 NFL Draft.

101. True. The Arizona Cardinals have only had the first overall pick once since 1980, and it was in 2019, when they drafted quarterback Kyler Murray.

102. Jerry Rice, who was drafted in the first round, 16th overall, by the San Francisco 49ers in the 1985 NFL Draft.

103. B. Joe Montana was picked in the third round, 82nd overall, of the 1979 NFL Draft.

104. False. Ronnie Lott was drafted eighth overall in the 1981 NFL Draft.

105. Brock Purdy.

106. Puka Nacua.

107. Devon Witherspoon.

CHAPTER 2
TEAMS

NAME THAT TEAM

108. The 1966 New York Giants.

109. The 1991 Indianapolis Colts (8.9 PPG) and the 1992 Seattle Seahawks (8.8 PPG).

110. The 2011 Oakland Raiders were assessed 163 penalties for 1,358 yards. That's 10 flags for 85 yards per game, on average.

111. The New Orleans Saints missed the playoffs from 1967 to 1986, a 20-year streak.

112. The Arizona Cardinals have not won a championship since 1947, a span that has seen the franchise play in Chicago as the Chicago Cardinals from 1922 to 1959, St. Louis as the St. Louis Cardinals from 1960 to 1987, and today in Phoenix as the Arizona Cardinals. They went from 1947 to 1998 without a playoff win.

113. The Dallas Cowboys, who did not have a losing season from 1966 to 1985, the longest such streak in NFL history.

114. The Pittsburgh Steelers had a 486–303–3 record from 1970 to 2020, giving them an NFL-best 61.6 win percentage, making them the only franchise that won at least 60 percent of their games over that time.

115. Despite winning 56.2 percent of their games, sixth best from 1970 to 2020, the Minnesota Vikings are the only franchise that was above .500 during that time to not win a Super Bowl title.

116. The Seattle Seahawks began their 43–8 Super Bowl XLVIII (48) win over the Denver Broncos with a safety, scoring faster than any team in Super Bowl history.

117. Devin Hester took the opening kickoff of Super Bowl XLI (41) for a touchdown against the Indianapolis Colts, giving the Chicago Bears the fastest six points in Super Bowl history.

118. The 1977 Atlanta Falcons allowed just 9.2 points per game.

119. The Baltimore Ravens allowed 10.3 points per game during their 2000 Super Bowl–winning season.

120. The Chicago Bears have retired 14 jersey numbers, the most in the NFL.

121. The Dallas Cowboys, the Atlanta Falcons, and the Raiders franchise do not believe in retiring jersey numbers. The Jacksonville Jaguars, the Baltimore Ravens, and the Houston Texans have also not retired any jersey numbers yet.

122. Since 1988, every NFL team has reached a conference championship game except the Houston Texans, who first started playing in 2002.

123. Helped out by O.J. Simpson's 2,003 yards in 1973, the Buffalo Bills became the first franchise to top the 3,000 rushing yards mark during an NFL season.

124. The Chicago Bears went undefeated in 1934 and 1942, but lost the NFL championship each time.

125. The Green Bay Packers won the NFL championship in 1929, 1930, and 1931, and then repeated the feat in 1965, 1966, and 1967, making them the only NFL franchise to ever three-peat.

126. The Miami Dolphins appeared in Super Bowl VI (6), VII (7), and VIII (8), losing the first game to the Dallas Cowboys, then winning the second against the Washington Commanders to complete their perfect season. They repeated as champions the next season with a win over the Minnesota Vikings.

127. The 2007 New England Patriots scored 589 points, breaking the record of 556 points set by the 1998 Minnesota Vikings. Each team saw Randy Moss play wide receiver and both teams fell short of winning a championship.

128. All six of the New England Patriots' Super Bowl wins were against teams with an animal nickname (St. Louis Rams, Carolina Panthers, Philadelphia Eagles, Seattle Seahawks, Atlanta Falcons, and Los Angeles Rams). In their five Super Bowl losses, they were defeated by the Chicago Bears, Philadelphia Eagles, Green Bay Packers, and the New York Giants … twice.

129. The Denver Broncos and the New England Patriots are tied for the record of most Super Bowl losses with five.

130. A. The Raiders' all-time leading passer is David Carr. Matt Schaub is the all-time leading passer of the Houston Texans.

131. Sam Cunningham, a first-round draft pick in 1973 out of USC, leads the New England Patriots with 5,453 rushing yards.

132. The Green Bay Packers have a .571 win percentage, making them the best in NFL history among active franchises.

133. As of the end of the 2023 NFL season, the Chicago Bears (793), Green Bay Packers (799), and New York Giants (721) are the only three NFL franchises with at least 700 regular season wins in their history.

134. Despite their two Super Bowl–winning seasons, the Tampa Bay Buccaneers entered 2023 with a .402 win percentage, the worst among all current NFL teams.

135. Ed Reed played with the Houston Texans in 2013, making him the only player in the Hall of Fame to have played for the franchise through the 2020 season.

136. The AFL/NFL merger was completed after Super Bowl IV (4), and since then the Miami Dolphins, Oakland Raiders, Denver Broncos, New England Patriots, and Kansas City Chiefs are the only AFL franchises to have won a Super Bowl championship.

137. Like MLB's Pirates and the NHL's Penguins, the Pittsburgh Steelers use black and gold as their team colors.

138. Along with their basic black, white, and silver, the Detroit Lions use Honolulu Blue as one of their uniform colors.

139. The New York Jets selected defensive end Shaun Ellis, defensive end John Abraham, quarterback Chad Pennington, and tight end Anthony Becht in the first round of the 2000 NFL Draft.

140. In 1997, the New England Patriots traded head coach Bill Parcells to the New York Jets for four draft picks. In 2000, the Jets traded Bill Belichick to the Patriots for three draft picks, but ended up sending back two of their own to New England.

141. The Buffalo Bills (Jim Kelly, Thurman Thomas, Andre Reed, Marv Levy), Indianapolis Colts (Peyton Manning, Edgerrin James, Marvin Harrison, Tony Dungy), and New York Jets (Joe Namath, Curtis Martin, Don Maynard, Weeb Ewbank) are the only three franchises to have their leading passer, rusher, receiver, and winningest head coach in the Hall of Fame.

142. The New Orleans Saints and the New York Jets won the Super Bowl in their only appearances, while the Baltimore Ravens and the Tampa Bay Buccaneers are two-for-two when playing for the title.

143. Known as the Redskins until 2020, the Washington franchise took the name Commanders in 2022 after two years as the Washington Football Team.

144. The Pittsburgh Steelers.

145. The San Franscisco 49ers.

GAMES WITH NICKNAMES

146. C. Baltimore Colts and New York Giants.

147. Dallas Cowboys and Green Bay Packers.

148. Buffalo Bills and Tennessee Titans.

149. Fog Bowl.

150. D. Dallas Cowboys and Philadelphia Eagles.

151. Philadelphia Eagles and New York Giants.

152. Buffalo Bills and Houston Oilers.

153. San Diego Chargers and Cincinnati Bengals.

154. Denver Broncos and Cleveland Browns.

155. Denver Broncos and Cleveland Browns. (This is not a typo. These two teams played in iconic back-to-back AFC Championship Games.)

MASCOTS AND LOGOS

156. Pat Patriot.

157. C. 1996

158. The Dallas Cowboys logo represents Texas as "The Lone Star State."

159. True.

160. Edgar Allen Poe. Poe is the Baltimore Ravens' mascot name.

161. 2000.

162. 2013.

163. McBeam.

164. Super Bowl XXXIII (33).

165. False. The Green Bay Packers don't have an official mascot. The current longest-running mascot in the NFL is that of the Atlanta Falcons, Freddie Falcon, who has been around for more than 35 years.

166. An elf.

167. 2004.

168. Two.

169. Bill Parcells.

170. A fleur-de-lis.

171. Seahawks are not a real bird; however, some people consider "sea hawks" to be a nickname for ospreys or skuas.

172. They are called the Raiders due to their original owner, Chet Soda, at first choosing the name "Señors" after holding a "name-the-team" contest. However, after fans were critical of the pick since Chet Soda called everyone "Señor," which put the validity and fairness of the contest in doubt, Chet Soda picked the runner-up name, the Raiders.

173. Purr.

174. Staley Da Bear is named after A. E. Staley, the man who originally founded the Bears franchise, in 1919.

175. Toro.

176. In 1919, the Green Bay team was sponsored by the Indian Packing Company, which is where team founder Earl "Curly" Lambeau first worked. In return for the sponsorship, the Indian Packing Company asked for the team to be nicknamed after them, and the Packers were born.

177. A Bucaneers are pirates, and the name is a nod to the pirates that raided Florida's coasts during the 17th century.

178. The Dolphin.

179. Bengal tigers are native to India and Bangladesh.

180. A St. Bernard puppy, which was based on a real puppy given to the New Orleans Saints by the Louisiana Restaurant Association in 1967 to serve as the team's mascot.

181. A winking buccaneer with a dagger between his teeth.

182. They are called the Jets due to the team playing near LaGuardia and JFK airports, and due to former owner David "Sonny" Werblin wanting the team to reflect a modern approach.

183. Direction. The Viking got turned from left to right.

184. They are called the Eagles due to owners Bert Bell and Lud Wray wanting to rename the Frankford Yellow Jackets in 1933 in honor of the symbol of the National Industrial Recovery Act, which was part of President Franklin D. Roosevelt's New Deal.

185. They are called the Giants due to the original team owner, Tim Mara, wanting to name his team after the Major League Baseball team the Giants, who were very popular at the time.

186. The Giants, Jets, Packers, and Chargers.

MOVES AND MERGERS

187. The Los Angeles Rams and the Baltimore Colts. In July 1972, the Los Angeles Rams saw owner Robert Irsay trade his team to Carroll Rosenbloom, who owned the Baltimore Colts.

188. The Rams franchise and the Cleveland Browns. The Rams franchise called Cleveland home from their founding in 1937 until 1945, before moving to Los Angeles. The next year, the Cleveland Browns were founded, and they played there until 1995 when the team was moved to Baltimore—but the Browns' stats and history stayed in Cleveland for when they were reborn in 1999.

189. The Steelers merged with the Philadelphia Eagles in 1943, going 5-4-1; the next year they merged with the Chicago Cardinals and went 0-10.

190. The AFL's Dallas Texans played from 1960 to 1962 before moving to Kansas City and becoming the Chiefs in 1963.

191. The Cardinals began playing in Chicago (1920 to 1959) before moving to St. Louis (1960 to 1987) and then Phoenix (1988 to present).

192. The Buffalo Bills play in Orchard Park, New York; the Los Angeles Chargers and Los Angeles Rams play in Inglewood, California; the Dallas Cowboys play in Arlington, Texas; the San Francisco 49ers play in Santa Clara, California; the New York Giants and the New York Jets play in East Rutherford, New Jersey; the Las Vegas Raiders play in Paradise, Nevada; and the Washington Commanders play in Landover, Maryland.

193. The Cleveland Browns, Baltimore Colts, and Pittsburgh Steelers all became AFC teams after the AFL/NFL merger.

194. The Washington Commanders called Boston home, and were known as the Boston Redskins from 1932 to 1936.

195. After Hurricane Katrina damaged the Superdome in 2005, the New Orleans Saints played one home game in the Giants Stadium, three in the Alamodome in San Antonio, and four others at Tiger Stadium on the campus of Louisiana State University. In 2010, after a snowfall damaged the roof of the Metrodome, the Minnesota Vikings played one home game at Detroit's Ford Field and another at TCF Bank Stadium on the University of Minnesota campus.

196. Portsmouth, Ohio, and they were called the Portsmouth Spartans.

FIELDS AND STADIUMS

197. Alltel Stadium, known today as TIAA Bank Field.

198. Ralph Wilson Stadium, known today as Highmark Stadium, was named after former owner Ralph Wilson.

199. Astrodome, which was home to the Houston Oilers from 1968 to 1996.

200. True. Soldier Field was built in 1924.

201. B. Carolina Panthers.

202. Cincinnati Bengals, Paul Brown Stadium.

203. 2002.

204. MetLife Stadium. Bonus trivia: Home to the New York Giants and the New York Jets, MetLife Stadium is actually in New Jersey.

205. Foxboro Stadium, known today as Gillette Stadium.

206. Veterans Stadium, which has since been demolished.

207. True.

208. A. $960,000.

209. Hard Rock Stadium opened in August of 1987.

210. RCA Dome, which has since been demolished.

211. FieldTurf.

212. Soldier Field, which seats 61,500 people.

213. Allegiant Stadium in Las Vegas, nicknamed the "Death Star".

THE OWNER'S BOX

214. The fans. The Green Bay Packers are a publicly traded entity.

215. 1989.

216. True. John Mara and Steve Tisch each own 50 percent of the team.

217. D. David Tepper, who owns the Carolina Panthers and has a net worth of over $2 billion.

218. 1994.

219. Jimmy Haslam, who owns the Cleveland Browns.

220. 1999.

221. Paul Allen, who owned the Seattle Seahawks.

222. Stan Kroenke, who owns the Los Angeles Rams.

223. Jim Irsay, who owns the Indianapolis Colts, and also owns a collection of more than 170 guitars, including David Gilmour's "Black Strat."

224. True. Amy Strunk's father, Bud Adams, was the founder of the Tennessee Titans.

225. Violet Bidwill Wolfner, who became the majority owner of the Chicago/St. Louis Cardinals, now known as the Arizona Cardinals.

226. George Halas, owner of the Chicago Bears from 1920 to 1983.

227. Lamar Hunt, owner of the Kansas City Chiefs from 1960 to 2006.

228. 1-C, 2-D, 3-E, 4-F, 5-A, 6-B.

229. Mark Davis.

230. The Denver Broncos.

CHAPTER 3
PLAYERS

NAME THAT PLAYER

231. Utah quarterback Alex Smith and USC running back Reggie Bush played together at Helix Charter High School in San Diego, and both received Heisman votes in 2004. Bush won the 2005 Heisman Trophy, but later had the award revoked for breaking NCAA rules.

232. Antonio Gates, who was a star basketball player at Kent State, had never played a single down of football in college before being given a tryout by the San Diego Chargers coming out of Kent State University.

233. Drew Brees and Nick Foles each attended Westlake High School in Austin, Texas.

234. In 1996, Larry Brown of the Dallas Cowboys became the first cornerback to win the MVP honor.

235. John Stallworth. Holmes won MVP in Super Bowl XLIII (43), Swan in Super Bowl X (10), and Ward in XL (40).

236. In Super Bowl VI (6), MVP Roger Staubach threw just 119 yards in the Dallas Cowboys' win over the Miami Dolphins, the fewest of any quarterback to win the award.

237. Chicago Bears linebacker Brian Urlacher played for the New Mexico Lobos in the late 1990s.

238. The Bears scored four rushing touchdowns in Super Bowl XX (20): two by quarterback Jim McMahon, one by fullback Matt

Suhey, and one by defensive lineman William Perry. Head coach Mike Ditka drew the ire of many football fans for shutting out Walter Payton during the game with his play calling.

239. Safety Kwamie Lassiter for the Arizona Cardinals against the San Diego Chargers on December 27, 1998; cornerback Deltha O'Neal for the Denver Broncos against the Kansas City Chiefs on November 7, 2001; and cornerback DeAngelo Hall for the Washington Commanders against the Chicago Bears October 24, 2010.

240. 49ers/Cowboys cornerback Deion Sanders in Super Bowl XXIX (29) and Super Bowl XXX (30), and Cowboys/49ers linebacker Ken Norton Jr. in Super Bowl XXVIII (28) and Super Bowl XXIX (29).

241. Detroit Lions kicker Jason Hanson with 2,150 points. He ranks fourth all-time in scoring, but is the top scorer among those who have only played for one franchise.

242. Kick returner Devin Hester scored 20 return touchdowns from 2006 to 2016, which broke the record held by Deion Sanders (1989 to 2005), whose career ended one year before Hester's began.

243. During the 2011 season, wide receiver Percy Harvin of the Minnesota Vikings took a kickoff out of the end zone and ran 104 yards without scoring a touchdown, setting the record for the longest return without scoring.

244. Linebacker Jack Ham is the only person enshrined in Canton, Ohio, to wear No. 59 during his pro career.

245. Joe Klecko of the New York Jets reached the Pro Bowl as a nose tackle, defensive end, and defensive tackle, and is the only player to reach the Pro Bowl from three different positions.

246. Cleveland's Jim Brown holds the record with eight career rushing titles, including five straight seasons from 1957 to 1961, leading the league in rushing yards. Brown later won three more titles from 1963 to 1965, setting the career record.

247. D, B, A, C. Testaverde had 46,223, Fouts had 43,040, Collins had 40,922, and Montana had 40,551.

248. Von Miller of the Denver Broncos majored in Poultry Science at Texas A&M University and has started the process of becoming a chicken farmer in his post-NFL career.

249. Justin Tucker of the Baltimore Ravens is a trained classical singer who has performed with the Baltimore Symphony Orchestra and New York City Opera, and can sing in seven languages.

250. The Washington Commanders placekicker Mark Moseley won the MVP award in the strike-shortened 1982 season. The last straight-ahead kicker, Moseley only missed one field goal that season. Washington went on to win the Super Bowl.

251. Tom Brady.

252. Peyton Manning.

253. Chargers running back LaDainian Tomlinson.

254. Steve Young.

255. Tom Brady and Ben Roethlisberger.

256. Ben Roethlisberger.

257. Baltimore Ravens kicker Justin Tucker.

258. Adrian Peterson, who recorded 296 rushing yards against the San Diego Chargers in 2007.

259. Oakland Raiders quarterback Daryle Lamonica.

260. Denver Broncos wide receiver Brandon Marshall, who had 21 receptions in 2009 against the Indianapolis Colts.

261. New Orleans Saints running back Alvin Kamara, who had six rushing touchdowns against the Minnesota Vikings in 2020.

262. Los Angeles Rams wide receiver Flipper Anderson, who had 336 receiving yards against the New Orleans Saints in 1989.

263. Buffalo Bills wide receiver Eric Moulds, who had 240 receiving yards against the Miami Dolphins in 1999.

264. Kansas City Chiefs defensive end Derrick Thomas, who had 7 sacks against the Seattle Seahawks in 1990.

265. New England Patriots outside linebacker Willie McGinest, who had 4.5 sacks against the Jacksonville Jaguars in 2006.

266. New York Jets linebacker David Harris, who recorded 20 solo tackles against the Washington Commanders in 2007.

267. Baltimore Ravens linebacker Ray Lewis, who had 156 solo tackles in 1997.

268. Buffalo Bills defensive end Bruce Smith, who ended his career with 200 sacks.

269. Pittsburgh Steelers cornerback Rod Woodson, who ended his career with 71 interceptions. Tunnel had 79 career interceptions, while Krause continues to hold the record with 81.

270. New England Patriots quarterback Tom Brady won in 2010 and Baltimore Ravens quarterback Lamar Jackson won in 2019.

271. Minnesota Vikings wide receiver Randy Moss.

272. Seattle Seahawks running back Marshawn Lynch.

273. Denver Broncos tight end Shannon Sharpe.

274. New York Giants linebacker Lawrence Taylor.

275. Cincinnati Bengals wide receiver Chad Ochocinco.

276. Cleveland Browns running back Jim Brown.

277. Dallas Cowboys quarterback Roger Staubach.

278. J.J. Watt (2012, 2014).

279. Indianapolis Colts wide receiver Marvin Harrison (1999, 2002).

280. Kansas City Chiefs linebacker Derrick Thomas.

281. Drew Brees and Tom Brady.

282. Michael Vick.

283. Cordarrelle Patterson.

284. Russell Wilson.

285. Deshaun Watson.

INNOVATORS

286. The Emmitt Smith Rule prohibits players from removing their helmet while on the field.

287. The Greg Pruitt Rule bans tear-away jerseys.

288. A rule that prohibits blindside blocks that come from the blocker's helmet, forearm, or shoulder, and land on the head or neck area of the defensive player.

289. The banning of Stickum, which was a substance used by players to improve their grip of the football.

290. Dallas Cowboys wide receiver Dez Bryant and Detroit Lions wide receiver Calvin Johnson.

291. Roughing the passer, which included the defender avoiding landing all or most of their body weight on a quarterback when taking him to the ground.

292. Pittsburgh's Mel Blount was well known for knocking down wide receivers crossing over the middle of Steelers defense until the "Mel Blount Rule" permitted just one "chuck" against receivers in the pass pattern.

293. The Nagurski to Grange pass was thrown less than five yards behind the line of scrimmage, which at the time was against the rules. The league soon changed the rule, allowing forward passes to take place from anywhere behind the line of scrimmage.

294. Before 1978, offensive linemen needed to pass block with a closed fist and their arm never extended. Nowadays, lineman can extend their hands and grab pass rushers as long as they don't reach outside the shoulder pads.

295. The "Immaculate Reception," by running back Franco Harris of the Pittsburgh Steelers, helped defeat the Oakland Raiders at the end of their 1972 AFC Playoff game. An existing rule that stipulated two offensive players could not touch a forward pass without a defender doing so in between them was strained by this play. The result was a rule change stating that anyone could catch and advance a "tipped pass," regardless of who else had touched it before.

296. The "forward fumble" by Oakland Raiders quarterback Ken Stabler was picked up by tight end Dave Kasper for an Oakland touchdown against the San Diego Chargers. The rule that resulted from this play is that only the player who fumbles from the offense can recover the ball in the last two minutes of each half, or on fourth down at any time during the game.

297. Chicago Cardinals cornerback Dick "Night Train" Lane, who influenced the creation of the facemask rule in 1956, because he was constantly grabbing offensive players by the facemask to take them down.

298. Los Angeles Rams defensive end Deacon Jones, who perfected the "head slap" and used it to beat offensive lineman consistently, which led to the NFL banning the move in 1977.

299. Cincinnati Bengals quarterback Carson Palmer.

300. The "Stroud Rule," which prohibits any player from leaping up to deflect a kick as it passes above the crossbar of a goal post.

301. The "Phil Dawson Rule" allows kicks that hit the uprights or crossbar to be reviewable.

302. Dallas Cowboys safety Roy Williams, who injured numerous players in 2004 using the horse-collar tackle, which led to it being banned in 2005.

303. Los Angeles Rams quarterback Norm Van Brocklin, who threw for 554 yards in 1951 against the New York Yanks.

304. NFL rule that was enacted in 2003 and declared a player's hair was an extension of his uniform and therefore fair game for tacklers.

305. Rule that prohibits any contact with a receiver beyond five yards from the line of scrimmage.

UNBELIEVABLE PLAYS

306. Wide receiver David Tyree, who made an unbelievable helmet catch while being defended by Patriots safety Rodney Harrison.

307. Cornerback Malcolm Butler, who made a game-sealing goal line interception.

308. Quarterback Nick Foles, who caught the touchdown pass from the Eagles tight end Trey Burton, who was pitched the ball by Eagles running back Corey Clement.

309. Tight end Dwight Clark, who made the game-winning touchdown reception from quarterback Joe Montana.

310. Running back Franco Harris, who made an unbelievable reception that came close to hitting the ground before Harris ran it in for the game-winning touchdown.

311. Safety Mike Davis, who intercepted the ball in the end zone, thus sealing the win for his team.

312. C. Quarterback Donovan McNabb, who completed a pass to wide receiver Freddie Mitchell for 28 yards.

313. Quarterback Mark Sanchez, who slid into guard Brandon Moore's rear end, and ended up fumbling. The ball was recovered by the New England Patriots and returned for a touchdown.

314. Miami Dolphins running back Kenyan Drake. The 2018 to 2019 Miami Dolphins team found a way to win the game with a lateral toss, even though they started at their own 31-yard line with seven seconds remaining in the game and trailing by five points.

315. B. Quarterback Dan Marino, who faked a spike, then threw the ball to wide receiver Mark Ingram for a touchdown to win the game.

316. Wide receiver DeSean Jackson, who had a game-winning punt return to end the game.

317. Quarterback John Elway, who was scrambling for a first down, had to leap over defenders and was hit in midair, which caused him to spin.

318. Tight end Dave Casper, who was nicknamed "Ghost" after Casper the Friendly Ghost.

319. Terrell Owens, who caught a 25-yard touchdown pass from Steve Young to seal the 49ers win over the Packers.

320. Running back Clarence Davis.

321. Wide receiver Odell Beckham Jr., who caught a one-handed fingertip touchdown while falling backward.

322. Wide receiver Stefon Diggs, who caught a 61-yard game-winning touchdown pass to advance to the NFC Championship Game.

323. Wide receiver Julian Edelman.

324. Quarterback Roger Staubach, who would throw up a long, low-probability pass with a very little chance of being completed.

325. Wide receiver Kevin Dyson, who received a lateral pass on a kickoff return with only seconds remaining in the game, and proceeded to return the ball 75 yards to score the winning touchdown.

FEUDS

326. Donovan McNabb.

327. Josh Norman.

328. Cortland Finnegan.

329. Aaron Rodgers.

330. Antonio Brown.

331. Sergio Brown.

332. Michael Crabtree.

333. Terrell Suggs.

334. Keyshawn Johnson.

335. Mike Vanderjagt.

336. Marcus Allen.

MOONLIGHTING

337. Deion Sanders.

338. Bo Jackson.

339. Tim Tebow.

340. False. Russell Wilson was the Colorado Rockies fourth-round draft pick in 2010.

341. True.

342. Brian Jordan.

343. C. Chris Hogan.

344. John Lynch.

345. Ricky Williams.

346. Drew Henson.

347. Mo-Alie Cox.

WHO SAID IT?

348. Wide receiver Terrell Owens.

349. Linebacker Ray Lewis.

350. Quarterback Terry Bradshaw.

351. Wide receiver Jerry Rice.

352. Wide receiver Steve Smith Sr.

353. Cornerback Deion Sanders.

354. Quarterback Joe Namath.

355. Tight end Rob Gronkowski.

356. Defensive tackle William "The Refrigerator" Perry.

357. Quarterback Joe Theismann.

358. Safety Jack Tatum.

359. Linebacker Dick Butkus.

360. Running back Eric Dickerson.

361. Quarterback Dan Marino.

362. Quarterback Tom Brady.

363. Running back Marshawn Lynch.

364. Running back Christian McCaffrey.

CHAPTER 4
COACHES

NAME THAT COACH

365. Antonio Pierce.

366. Kevin Stefanski.

367. Vince Lombardi, who has a .900 winning percentage in the playoffs.

368. Don Shula, who led all coaches with 328 regular season wins at the end of 2020.

369. Andy Reid, who won 100 games for the Philadelphia Eagles and Kansas City Chiefs.

370. Tony Dungy.

371. B. Don Shula, who has won four NFL Coach of the Year awards.

372. Bill Belichick, who has six Super Bowl wins with the New England Patriots (2002, 2004, 2005, 2015, 2017, and 2019).

373. Tom Landry, who had 20 consecutive winning seasons.

374. Tom Coughlin.

375. George Halas, who was a head coach for 40 years in the NFL.

376. Bill Belichick, who has coached in 43 playoff games (as of 2023).

377. Don Shula.

378. Vince Lombardi, who won Super Bowls I (1) and II (2).

379. New England Patriots coach Bill Belichick with six and Pittsburgh Steelers coach Chuck Noll with four.

380. Fritz Pollard.

381. Coach Bill Walsh, who invented the offense while he was quarterbacks coach for the Cincinnati Bengals.

382. Dallas Cowboys head coach Tom Landry.

383. Romeo Crennel, who served as head coach at the age of 73.

384. Mike Singletary, who won the Man of the Year award as a player in 1990.

385. George Halas.

386. C. John Madden, who had a .759 winning percentage during the regular season.

387. Bill Parcells, who won the Coach of the Year award with the New York Giants and New England Patriots.

388. Joe Gibbs, who won the Coach of the Year award in 1982 and 1983 with the Washington Commanders.

389. Chuck Knoll.

390. New Orleans Saints head coach Sean Payton, who played for the Chicago Bruisers and Pittsburgh Gladiators.

391. Andy Reid.

392. John Harbaugh.

393. Joe Gibbs, who won Super Bowls with Joe Theismann, Doug Williams, and Mark Rypien.

394. Mike Ditka.

395. Tom Flores.

396. Jimmy Johnson.

397. Chicago Bears head coach George Halas.

398. Jim Harbaugh and John Harbaugh.

399. Chuck Knox.

400. New Orleans Saints head coach Sean Payton and defensive coordinator Gregg Williams.

401. Sean McVay, who became a head coach at the age of 30.

402. Tom Landry.

403. Bill Parcells, who led the New York Giants (1984, 1985, 1986, 1989, 1990), New England Patriots (1994, 1996), New York Jets (1998), and Dallas Cowboys (2003, 2006) to the playoffs.

404. Marty Schottenheimer, who has 200 wins.

405. Sal Alosi, who tripped Miami Dolphins cornerback Nolan Carroll.

406. Mike Tomlin.

407. John Ralston.

408. Don Coryell.

409. St. Louis Rams head coach Dick Vermeil.

410. Hank Bullough.

411. Lovie Smith.

412. Jeff Saturday, who did not return in 2023.

413. Nathaniel Hackett.

414. Paul Brown, Pete Carroll, Jimmy Johnson, and Barry Switzer.

415. John Madden.

COACHING TREES

416. Bill Belichick.

417. Sean Payton.

418. Indianapolis Colts' Tony Dungy (Super Bowl XLI (41)), Tampa Bay Buccaneers' Bruce Arians (Super Bowl LV (55)), Green Bay Packers' Mike McCarthy (Super Bowl XLV (45)), and Pittsburgh Steelers' Bill Cowher (Super Bowl XL (40)).

419. Pittsburgh Steelers' Mike Tomlin (Super Bowl XLIII (43)), Chicago Bears' Lovie Smith (Super Bowl XLI (41)), and Indianapolis Colts' Jim Caldwell (Super Bowl XLIV (44)).

420. Dick LeBeau.

421. Arizona Cardinals head coach Buddy Ryan, who had his twin sons Rex Ryan (D-line and linebackers coach) and Rob Ryan (defensive backs coach) on his coaching staff.

422. University of Alabama head coach Nick Saban.

423. Head coach Mike Shanahan and offensive coordinator Kyle Shanahan.

424. Mike Ditka, who won Super Bowl XX (20) with the Chicago Bears.

425. Los Angeles Rams head coach Sean McVay (Super Bowl LIII (53)) and San Francisco 49ers head coach Kyle Shanahan (Super Bowl LIV (54)).

426. Kansas City Chiefs head coach Andy Reid (Super Bowl LIV (54)) and former Tampa Bay Buccaneers head coach Jon Gruden (Super Bowl XXXVII (37)).

427. John Harbaugh.

428. Bum Phillips (head coach) and Wade Phillips (defensive line and defensive coordinator).

429. B. Paul Brown.

430. Seattle Seahawks head coach Mike Holmgren and San Francisco 49ers head coach George Seifert.

431. Andy Reid.

432. Bill Walsh.

433. Bill Walsh.

434. Andy Reid.

435. Dick Vermeil.

INNOVATORS

436. New England Patriots' trick play vs. Baltimore Ravens during the 2014 AFC divisional playoff round, which resulted in key first downs for the Patriots.

437. Quarterback communication via helmets.

438. Green Bay Packers head coach Vince Lombardi.

439. Arizona Cardinals head coach Bruce Arians, who hired Jennifer Welter as a coaching intern in 2015.

440. Cincinnati Bengals head coach Sam Wyche.

441. San Diego Chargers head coach Sid Gillman.

442. Tampa Bay Buccaneers head coach Tony Dungy and defensive coordinator Monte Kiffin.

443. St. Louis Rams head coach Jeff Fisher, who drafted defensive end Michael Sam in 2014.

444. Cleveland Browns head coach Paul Brown.

445. Kansas City Chiefs head coach Hank Stram.

446. Buddy Ryan.

FEUDS

447. Quarterback Tom Brady.

448. Dallas Cowboys owner Jerry Jones.

449. D. Detroit Lions head coach Jim Schwartz.

450. New York Jets head coach Eric Mangini.

451. New England Patriots owner Robert Kraft.

452. Defensive coordinator Buddy Ryan.

453. Los Angeles Raiders owner Al Davis.

454. Houston Oilers offensive coordinator Kevin Gilbride.

455. Denver Broncos offensive coordinator Mike Shanahan.

456. Houston Oilers head coach Jerry Glanville.

WHO SAID IT

457. San Francisco 49ers' Mike Singletary.

458. C. Oakland Raiders' Bill Callahan.

459. Arizona Cardinals' Dennis Green.

460. New York Jets' Herm Edwards.

461. Indianapolis Colts' Jim Mora.

462. B. New England Patriots' Bill Parcells.

463. A. New England Patriots' Bill Belichick.

464. Tampa Bay Buccaneers' John Mckay.

465. New England Patriots' Bill Belichick.

466. B. New York Jets' Rex Ryan.

467. A. Oakland Raiders' John Madden.

468. D. New England Patriots' Bill Belichick.

469. Houston Oilers' Bill Peterson.

470. Cincinnati Bengals' Bruce Coslet.

471. Denver Broncos' Wade Phillips.

472. Detroit Lions' Dan Campbell.

473. Seahawks' Pete Carroll.

474. Jets' Robert Saleh.

CHAPTER 5
SUPER BOWL

MEMORABLE MOMENTS

475. B. Sean Payton of the New Orleans Saints began the second half of Super Bowl XLIV (44) with an onside kick against the Indianapolis Colts, which the Saints secured, and ultimately helped them win the game.

476. Chicago Bears kick returner Devin Hester, who returned the opening kickoff for a touchdown in Super Bowl XLI (41).

477. The Washington Commanders scored 35 points in the second quarter against the Denver Broncos in Super Bowl XXII (22).

478. Indiana (Super Bowl XLVI (46)) and New Jersey (Super Bowl XLVII (47)) each have hosted the Super Bowl once.

479. Scott Norwood's 47-yard field goal attempt went wide right in Super Bowl XXV (25).

480. St. Louis Rams' linebacker Mike Jones tackled Tennessee Titans' wide receiver Kevin Dyson one yard short of a potential game-winning touchdown in Super Bowl XXXIV (34).

481. The Baltimore Ravens were leading 28–6 over the San Francisco 49ers early in the third quarter when the lights in the Louisiana Superdome went out, causing a 34-minute delay.

482. Miami Dolphins placekicker Garo Yepremian had a 42-yard field goal attempt blocked by the Washington Commanders in Super Bowl VII (7). Yepremian tried to throw a pass after the kick was blocked, but Washington intercepted the pass for a pick-six. The final score was 14–7, Miami.

483. Carolina Panthers kicker John Kasay tied Super Bowl XXXVIII (38) at 29 points with a late field goal. On the following kickoff, he whiffed the ball out of bounds, giving the New England Patriots possession at their 40-yard line with 1:08 left in the game. New England quarterback Tom Brady drove down the field and the Patriots kicked a game-winning field goal.

484. After defensive tackle Leon Lett recovered a fumble and was well on his way to giving the Dallas Cowboys a six-touchdown lead, wide receiver Don Beebe caught the defensive lineman from behind and knocked the ball out of the end zone, giving the ball back to the Buffalo Bills.

485. Seattle Seahawks wide receiver Ricardo Lockette was the intended receiver of quarterback Russell Wilson's pass, which was intercepted by New England Patriots Malcom Butler. The Patriots won Super Bowl XLIX (49) 28–24.

486. Linebacker James Harrison of the Pittsburgh Steelers intercepted Kurt Warner of the St. Louis Rams and returned the pass for a touchdown. Rather than seeing the Rams tie or take the lead, the play gave the Steelers a 17–7 lead at halftime of Super Bowl XLIII (43) in a game they would win 27–23.

487. An admittedly hungover Max McGee caught a 37-yard pass from Green Bay Packers quarterback Bart Starr as part of his 137-yard, two-touchdown Super Bowl I (1) performance. The one-handed catch will always be known as the first touchdown in Super Bowl history.

488. David Tyree made his fourth-down "Helmet Catch" in Super Bowl XLII (42) and Mario Manningham made a 38-yard sideline catch in Super Bowl XLV (45).

489. Antwaan Randle El become the first wide receiver to throw a Super Bowl touchdown pass when he found Pittsburgh Steelers teammate Hines Ward for a 43-yard score in Super Bowl XL (40).

490. Super Bowl XII (12) in the Louisiana Superdome was the first to be played on artificial turf.

491. San Francisco 49ers quarterback Joe Montana reportedly pointed out actor John Candy in the stands prior to leading a 92-yard, game-winning drive in Super Bowl XXIII (23) against the Cincinnati Bengals.

492. In Super Bowl XXIX (29), wide receiver Jerry Rice caught three touchdown passes, while teammate running back Ricky Watters caught two and ran for a third touchdown in the 49–26 rout of the San Diego Chargers.

493. Running back Thurman Thomas of the Buffalo Bills missed the first two plays of Super Bowl XXVI (26) after his helmet was moved during the pregame festivities.

494. The Chicago Bears hoisted both head coach Mike Ditka and defensive coordinator Buddy Ryan off the field after their 46–10 win in Super Bowl XX (20) against the New England Patriots.

495. The "Philly Special" was a handoff from Philadelphia Eagles quarterback Nick Foles to running back Corey Clement, who then pitched it to tight end Trey Burton. It was a pass by Burton back to a wide open Foles in the end zone that gave the Eagles a 22–12 lead in Super Bowl LII (52), and ultimately helped them to a 41–33 win.

496. New England Patriots running back James White scored the first overtime touchdown in Super Bowl history with a rushing touchdown in Super Bowl LI (51).

497. Late in Super Bowl XLIV (54), New Orleans Saints cornerback Tracy Porter intercepted Indianapolis Colts quarterback Peyton Manning. Porter turned the interception into a pick-six to secure New Orleans' 31–17 win, giving the franchise their first-ever Super Bowl win.

498. After a Baltimore Ravens touchdown in Super Bowl XXXV (35), wide receiver Ron Dixon of the New York Giants returned the kickoff for a touchdown. Wide receiver Jermaine Lewis responded for the Ravens with a touchdown return of his own on the ensuing kickoff, which ultimately helped the Ravens win 34–7.

499. Denver Broncos running back Terrell Davis was allowed to score a touchdown against the Green Bay Packers defense at the instruction of head coach Mike Holmgren, who wanted to preserve time on the clock. The Packers were unable to mount a comeback and lost Super Bowl XXXII (32) 31–24.

500. Veteran tight end Jackie Smith was called upon to catch a pass from quarterback Roger Staubach in Super Bowl XIII (13), but dropped the pass despite being wide open, forcing the Cowboys to settle for a field goal. The Pittsburgh Steelers went on to win the game 35–31.

501. Placekicker Jim O'Brien of the Baltimore Colts won Super Bowl V (5) with a field goal, helping defeat the Dallas Cowboys 16–13.

502. William "The Refrigerator" Perry helped the Chicago Bears defeat the New England Patriots 46–10 in Super Bowl XX (20) when the defensive lineman scored a fourth quarter rushing touchdown.

503. Running back John Riggins scampered 43 yards on a fourth-and-one fourth quarter play to help give the Washington Commanders a three-point lead over the Miami Dolphins. Washington would win Super Bowl XVII (17) 27–17, with Riggins winning MVP honors.

504. Quarterback Joe Namath left the field after Super Bowl III (3) with his index finger waving in the air after the New York Jets upset the heavily favored Baltimore Colts.

505. John Madden was doubtful about a young quarterback named Tom Brady going for the win against the St. Louis Rams in Super Bowl XXXVI (36), insisting the New England Patriots take their chances in overtime. The Pats won 20–17 in regulation.

506. Donovan McNabb was reportedly vomiting in the Philadelphia Eagles huddle during Super Bowl XXXIX (39). As a result, head coach Andy Reid could not run a hurry-up offense while down 24–21, and the Eagles were limited to one late drive, which fell short, costing the Eagles a chance to tie.

507. After jumping out to a 20–0 halftime lead, the San Francisco 49ers were up 20–7 in Super Bowl XVI (16) against the Cincinnati Bengals in the third quarter. With momentum building, a drive put the Bengals on the three-yard line; but the 49ers' defense held without allowing a touchdown. The sequence proved important since the final score was 26–21, San Francisco.

508. After winning Super Bowl XII (12) over the Denver Broncos, Dallas Cowboys head coach Tom Landry was carried off the field. However, it was Dion Rich, a notorious gatecrasher of the time, who carried the well-dressed Landry off the floor of the Louisiana Superdome.

509. New York Giants' quarterback Phil Simms was the first MVP to utter the phrase "I'm going to Disney World," which he did after winning Super Bowl XXI (21) over the Denver Broncos.

510. Travis Kelce (Kansas City) and Jason Kelce (Philadelphia).

RECORD HOLDERS

511. Terrell Davis of the Denver Broncos is the only running back to score three touchdowns, doing so in Super Bowl XXXII (32) against the Green Bay Packers.

512. San Francisco 49ers wide receiver Jerry Rice scored three receiving touchdowns in both Super Bowl XXIV (24) against the Denver Broncos and Super Bowl XXIX (29) against the San Diego Chargers.

513. Timmy Smith of the Washington Commanders posted 204 rushing yards in Super Bowl XXII (22) against the Denver Broncos. It was the first time Smith had ever started an NFL game at running back.

514. Aided by a 58-yard run, running back Tom Matte of the Baltimore Colts posted 116 yards on 11 carries (a 10.5-yard average) in Super Bowl III (3) against the New York Jets.

515. In Super Bowl XXXVII (37), Oakland Raiders quarterback Rich Gannon was picked off a record five times by the Tampa Bay Buccaneers' defense.

516. During five Super Bowl appearances, Denver Broncos' quarterback John Elway threw eight interceptions.

517. Quarterback Gale Gilbert was on the Buffalo Bills when they lost Super Bowl XXII (22), XXIII (23), XXV (25), and XXVI (26), and was also on the San Diego Chargers when they lost Super Bowl XXIX (29).

518. Ken Norton Jr. was part of the Dallas Cowboys back-to-back Super Bowl wins (XXVII (27) and XXVIII (28)), and then joined the San Francisco 49ers and won Super Bowl XXIX (29). He was the first player to win two straight titles with two different teams and is the only player to be part of three consecutive Super Bowl wins.

519. Hall of Fame Washington Commanders head coach Joe Gibbs tallied three Super Bowl victories, each with a different quarterback: Joe Theismann (Super Bowl XVII (17)), Doug Williams (Super Bowl XXII (22)), and Mark Rypien (Super Bowl XXVI (26)).

520. Kicker Jim Turner (Super Bowl III (3)) and kicker Mike Clark (Super Bowl VI (6)) each kicked a nine-yard field goal, something which is no longer possible, since the goalposts are now at the back of the end zone. This ensures each kicker will have the record for the shortest field goals in Super Bowl history.

521. Defensive end L.C. Greenwood recorded four sacks against the Dallas Cowboys, helping the "Steel Curtain" defense of the Pittsburgh Steelers win Super Bowl X (10), 21–17.

522. Charles Haley played linebacker and defensive end for the Dallas Cowboys and the San Francisco 49ers, and became the first player to win five Super Bowl rings.

523. Jake Moody kicked a then-record 55-yard field goal in Super Bowl LVIII (53). This record was broken when Kansas City Chief Harrison Butker kicked a 57-yard field goal the next quarter.

524. D. As part of the Pittsburgh Steelers' Super Bowl XL (40) win, quarterback Ben Roethlisberger was 23 years and 340 days old, making him the youngest quarterback to ever win a Super Bowl.

525. A. Head coach Mike Tomlin was 36 years and 341 days old when the Pittsburgh Steelers captured Super Bowl XLIII (43).

526. On the final play of the first quarter in Super Bowl VI (6), Miami Dolphins quarterback Bob Griese took the snap from his own 38 yard-line. Facing a relentless pass rush from the Dallas Cowboys, Griese ran away from the line of scrimmage before being sacked by defensive tackle Bob Lilly for a record 29-yard loss.

527. After scoring a defensive safety 12 seconds into Super Bowl XLVIII (48), the Seattle Seahawks never trailed the Denver Broncos in their 43–8 rout, leading for the remaining 59:48 of the game.

528. Tom Brady threw for 505 yards in Super Bowl LII (52), but it wasn't enough for the New England Patriots to defeat the Philadelphia Eagles, who prevailed 41–33.

529. When the New England Patriots defeated the Los Angeles Rams 13–3 in Super Bowl LIII (53), they became the lowest-scoring team to win a Super Bowl. Ironically, the 10-point margin of victory is the largest among the Patriots' six Super Bowl wins.

530. The Super Bowl LVIII (53) matchup between the winning Kansas City Chiefs and the San Francisco 49ers was reportedly watched by 123.7 million viewers, the most of any television broadcast.

531. Tom Flores won two Super Bowls as a head coach with the Oakland/Los Angeles Raiders and a Super Bowl as a player with the Kansas City Chiefs. The other former players who won Super Bowls as a player and head coach are Mike Ditka (as a tight end of the Dallas Cowboys and head coach of the Chicago Bears), Tony Dungy (as a safety of the Pittsburgh Steelers and head coach of the Indianapolis Colts) and Doug Pederson (as a quarterback of the Green Bay Packers and head coach of the Philadelphia Eagles).

532. 65 yards.

533. Minnesota Vikings.

DYNASTIES

534. The San Francisco 49ers won their first five Super Bowls before losing their next two.

535. The New York Giants are 4–1 in the Super Bowl, but have scored and allowed 104 points.

536. The Pittsburgh Steelers (coaches: Chuck Noll, Bill Cowher, and Mike Tomlin; quarterbacks: Terry Bradshaw and Ben Roethlisberger) and the Dallas Cowboys (coaches: Tom Landry, Jimmy Johnson, and Barry Switzer; quarterbacks: Roger Staubach and Troy Aikman) each have three head coaches who have won the Super Bowl, but only two quarterbacks.

537. Brett Favre won Super Bowl XXXI (31), but Desmond Howard won MVP honors that year, making Favre the only Packers quarterback to win a ring but not the MVP.

538. Kerry Collins is the only New York Giants quarterback to start and lose a Super Bowl. Collins started Super Bowl XXXV (35) and failed to put any offensive points on the scoreboard, losing to the Baltimore Ravens 34–7.

539. The San Francisco 49ers won Super Bowl XXIII (23) with Bill Walsh as their head coach, who retired after winning his third title. They then won Super Bowl XXIV (24) with George Seifert as their head coach, Seifert's first of two championships (second was Super Bowl XXIX (29)) with two different quarterbacks (Joe Montana and Steve Young).

540. Herschel Walker.

541. Wide receiver Deion Branch (Super Bowl XXXIX (39)) and wide receiver Julian Edelman (Super Bowl LIII (53)) are the only two New England Patriots other than Tom Brady to win Super Bowl MVP honors.

542. The Pittsburgh Steelers and Dallas Cowboys have played each other for a championship three times, with the Steelers winning

Super Bowls X (10) and XIII (13) and the Cowboys winning Super Bowl XXX (30).

543. The Green Bay Packers won Super Bowl I (1) and Super Bowl XLV (45) without playing a single playoff game at Lambeau Field. Four other teams have won a single Super Bowl without playing any postseason games at home: The Kansas City Chiefs (IV) (4), Pittsburgh Steelers (XL) (40), New York Giants (XLII) (42), and Tampa Bay Buccaneers (LV) (50).

544. The Pittsburgh Steelers won their first four Super Bowls in a six-year span by capturing Super Bowls IX (9), X (10), XIII (13), and XIV (14). They are the only franchise with a pair of back-to-back Super Bowl wins.

545. In 1969, the Pittsburgh Steelers hired Chuck Noll as their head coach. They next hired Bill Cowher in 1992, and then Mike Tomlin in 2007; all three have won at least one Super Bowl.

546. Tony Easton (Super Bowl XX (20)), Drew Bledsoe (Super Bowl XXXI (31)), and Tom Brady (Super Bowls XLII (42), XLVI (46), LII (52)) are the three starting quarterbacks to lose a Super Bowl.

547. Chuck Noll went 4–0 in Super Bowls with the Pittsburgh Steelers, while Bill Walsh went 3–0 with the San Francisco 49ers.

548. B. The San Francisco 49ers, who scored 55 points in Super Bowl XXIV (24) against the Denver Broncos.

COMMERCIAL BREAKS

549. Apple used Super Bowl XVIII (18) in January 1984 to launch an ad campaign for their new Macintosh personal computer.

550. In 1993, a McDonald's commercial featured Larry Bird and Michael Jordan playing a game of Horse and gave fans the catchphrase "nothing but net."

551. The Budweiser Clydesdale horses played a game of football in 2003 and asked a Zebra to be their replay review referee.

552. Coca-Cola's famous "Hey Kid, Catch!" commercial featured defensive tackle "Mean" Joe Greene of the Pittsburgh Steelers limping toward the locker room when a young fan hands Greene a soda bottle. As thanks for the Coca-Cola, Greene tosses the fan his game jersey.

553. Ali Landry starred in several Super Bowl XXXII (32) commercials for Frito Lay and earned the name the "Doritos Girl" after several steamy segments highlighted the ads in 1998.

554. Enlisting the likes of Danica Patrick as "GoDaddy Girls," GoDaddy.com ran risqué ads that pushed the limits of Super Bowl censors, leaving the company to air "teaser" ads during the game and post the uncensored commercials on their website.

555. Tim Tebow, drafted by the Denver Broncos, and his mother, Pam, appeared in a Super Bowl XLIV (44) ad for a group called "Focus on the Family" that told the story of how doctors didn't think the quarterback would be born alive after Pam was diagnosed with a dangerous medical condition while pregnant.

556. Super Bowl XVIII (18) saw Wendy's roll out their "Where's the Beef," commercials highlighting their hamburgers had more meat than those served at McDonald's or Burger King.

557. Noxzema hired New York Jets quarterback Joe Namath to promote their shaving cream for Super Bowl VII (7) with future *Charlie's Angels* actress Farrah Fawcett applying the product to his face.

558. The E*Trade "Baby" was a popular commercial during Super Bowl XLII (42).

559. Michael Jackson famously burned his hair while filming a Pepsi commercial, but not before starring in a 90-second spot in 1984 during Super Bowl XVIII (18).

560. Michael Jordan starred with "Hare Jordan," aka Bugs Bunny, in a Nike ad during Super Bowl XXVI (26). It was this popular pairing that led to more commercials and the first *Space Jam* movie.

561. Snickers had one of the most highly rated Super Bowl ads in 2010, when they had Betty White star in their Super Bowl XLIV (44) commercial.

562. As Paralympic star Amy Purdy trains, the iconic voice of Muhammad Ali provided the poetic background sound with his "Handcuffed Lightning and Thrown Thunder in Jail" speech during a Toyota commercial that pitches an idea, not their car.

563. Bud, Weis, and Er.

564. FTX.

565. Ben Affleck.

MVPS

566. Quarterback Phil Simms (Super Bowl XXI (21)), quarterback Mark Rypien (Super Bowl XXVI (26)), and wide receiver Julian Edelman (Super Bowl LIII (53)) are the three Super Bowl MVPs who wore jersey No. 11 for their team.

567. Quarterbacks Joe Namath (Super Bowl III (3)), Roger Staubach (Super BowlVI (6)), Terry Bradshaw (XIII (13) and XIV (14)), Tom Brady (five times), and Aaron Rodgers (XLV (45)) all won the Super Bowl MVP wearing No. 12 for their team.

568. C. Defensive end Richard Dent of the Chicago Bears wore No. 95 when he earned Super Bowl XX (20) MVP honors.

569. Quarterback Eli Manning of the New York Giants (Super Bowl XLII (42)) and wide receiver Santonio Holmes of the Pittsburgh Steelers (Super Bowl XLIII (43)) each won Super Bowl MVP while wearing No. 10.

570. Ottis Anderson of the New York Giants won Super Bowl XXV (25) honors, but has yet to join fellow running backs Larry Csonka (of the Miami Dolphins), Franco Harris (of the Pittsburgh Steelers), John Riggins (of the Washington Commanders), Marcus Allen (of the Los Angeles Raiders), Emmitt Smith (of the Dallas Cowboys), and Terrell Davis (of the Denver Broncos) in the Pro Football Hall of Fame.

571. The Pittsburgh Steelers have seen quarterback Terry Bradshaw (twice), running back Franco Harris, and wide receivers Hines Ward and Santonio Holmes win the Super Bowl MVP. They were matched by the Oakland/Los Angeles Raiders, who saw wide receiver Fred Biletnikoff, quarterback Jim Plunkett, and running back Marcus Allen each capture a Super Bowl MVP award.

572. Mark Rypien (Super Bowl XXVI (26)), who was born in Canada, and Hines Ward (Super Bowl XL (40)), who was born in South Korea.

573. A. After jumping out 14–0 over the Cincinnati Bengals in Super Bowl XVI (16), the San Francisco 49ers' offense stalled on four drives and had to settle for field goals. With a final score of 26–21 in favor of the 49ers, some feel placekicker Ray Wersching and not quarterback Joe Montana deserved MVP honors.

574. Dallas Cowboys linebacker Chuck Howley, who was named MVP of Super Bowl V (5).

575. B. Joe Namath of the New York Jets only threw for 206 yards and no touchdowns in Super Bowl III (3), leaving many to think that running back Matt Snell, who had 30 carries for 121 yards, should have been named the game's MVP.

576. True. Since Super Bowl XXXV (35) played in January 2001, a cornerback, three linebackers, four wide receivers, and eight different quarterbacks have won Super Bowl MVP honors. Seven running backs were named Super Bowl MVP prior to Super Bowl XXXV (35).

577. Kurt Warner (Super Bowl XXXIV (34)) had 414 passing yards and Tom Brady (Super Bowl LI (51)) had 466 yards.

578. False. Fred Biletnikoff of the Oakland Raiders won the Super Bowl XI (11) MVP with only four catches and 79 yards while failing to score a touchdown.

579. Dallas Cowboys defensive end Harvey Martin and defensive tackle Randy White, who were named Co-MVPs of Super Bowl XII (7).

580. The Miami Dolphins. Safety Jake Scott and running back Larry Csonka won the MVP in the Dolphins' two Super Bowl wins.

581. Eight: quarterback, linebacker, safety, running back, wide receiver, defensive end, cornerback, kick returner.

582. Tom Brady (7), Joe Montana (4), Terry Bradshaw (4), and Troy Aikman (3).

CHAPTER 6
BLOOPERS AND SURPRISES

NFL WTF?

583. Detroit Lions wide receiver Calvin Johnson had a touchdown reversed and changed to an incompletion, as he was said to have not completed the process of a catch.

584. C. Snowplow.

585. Tails, Heads.

586. The referee said Jerry Rice was down by contact even though he had fumbled the ball.

587. Defensive end Dee Ford.

588. Wide receiver Dez Bryant made a catch and, while he attempted to extend the ball for the goal line to score a touchdown, the ball touched the ground, which turned the catch into an incompletion.

589. Illegal Forward Lateral.

590. Personal Foul. New Orleans Saints defensive end Bobby McCray took a direct shot at the back of Green Bay Packers quarterback Brett Favre's leg, yet no foul was called.

591. "The Tuck Rule," which ruled that Tom Brady did not fumble after a strip sack, but instead had an incomplete pass due to his arm going forward to bring the ball back into his stomach.

592. Giants guard Rich Seubert was flagged for illegal man downfield even though he checked in as an eligible receiver.

593. A. Touchdown.

594. Jerry Rice lost the ball out the back of the end zone before crossing back over the goal line, which should have resulted in a touchback; however, the referees still called it a touchdown.

595. D. Helmet.

596. John Taylor dropped the ball at the goal line as he was trying to catch it, yet the referees ruled it a touchdown.

597. After the Cleveland Browns had snapped the ball on a first down, referees reviewed the previous fourth-down play and changed the call from a completed pass to an incompletion, even though the play was ineligible for review. The Browns would lose the game 15–10.

598. A. Houchli's erroneous call resulted in the Denver Broncos retaining possession of the ball, and the Broncos eventually scoring the game-winning touchdown.

599. Super Bowl XL (40), Seahawks vs. Steelers. Among many controversial calls was an offensive pass interference call on Seattle Seahawks wide receiver Darrell Jackson, which nullified his touchdown.

600. Houston Oilers wide receiver Mike Renfro.

601. Pass Interference, where Rams cornerback Nickell Robey-Coleman hit Saints wide receiver Tommylee Lewis well before the ball arrived in a tied 20–20 game with 1:49 left in the fourth quarter.

602. A fourth quarter interception by the Jets was confirmed even though replays showed the Lions' defender was out of bounds. There were no instant replay reviews at the time.

603. Unsportsmanlike Conduct Penalty.

604. Offensive Pass Interference, where Cowboys wide receiver Drew Pearson pushed off of Minnesota Vikings cornerback Nate Wright.

605. Uncalled Holding/Pass Interference by NaVorro Bowman on Roddy White in the end zone, on fourth down with a minute left in the game. Had the foul been called, the Falcons would have taken possession of the ball at the one-yard line and had an opportunity to win the game.

606. Wide receiver Jerricho Cotchery bobbled a ball, yet it never touched the ground. However, the referees ruled the play an incomplete pass, even after replays showed the ball never hit the ground.

607. Pittsburgh Steelers wide receiver Santonio Holmes' game-winning touchdown catch, specifically if his right foot touched down or if his toes were pressed against his left cleat. After a booth review, the play stood as called.

608. The Miami Dolphins.

609. Marvin Jones.

FANS GONE WILD

610. Green Bay Packers quarterback Brett Favre.

611. Junior Seau, who was tackled after the fan attempted to give him a hug.

612. New England Patriots quarterback Tom Brady.

613. A snowball.

614. Chicago Bears safety Corey Graham.

615. Pittsburgh Steelers outside linebacker James Harrison.

616. Kansas City Chiefs wide receiver Tyreek Hill.

617. New York Jets defensive end Shaun Ellis.

618. Oakland Raiders offensive tackle Lincoln Kennedy.

619. Dallas Cowboys running back Ezekiel Elliott.

620. New England Patriots linebacker Matt Chatham.

621. Pittsburgh Steelers quarterback Ben Roethlisberger.

622. Dallas Cowboys wide receiver Michael Irvin.

623. Denver Broncos quarterback John Elway.

624. Dallas Cowboys wide receiver Terrell Owens.

625. San Diego Chargers.

MUSICAL MEMORIES

626. "The Super Bowl Shuffle."

627. Running back LaDainian Tomlinson.

628. True. Terry Bradshaw's version of "I'm So Lonesome I Could Cry," off his 1976 album of the same name, peaked at No. 91 on the Billboard Hot 100.

629. Marc Colombo, Leonard Davis, and Cory Procter.

630. "Must Be the Money."

631. Danny White, who played with the Cowboys from 1976 to 1988.

632. "Fortune and Pain."

633. "Let It Shine."

634. Le'Veon Bell.

635. Cole Beasley.

BLOOPERS AND FLUBS

636. DeSean Jackson, in a 2008 game against the Dallas Cowboys.

637. Tampa Bay Buccaneers quarterback Jameis Winston.

638. Tony Romo, who botched the snap in the wildcard playoff game between the Dallas Cowboys and Seattle Seahawks.

639. The Detroit Lions' Dan Orlovsky.

640. Darius Reynaud, who committed a safety on the first kickoff of the 2013 season.

641. Sage Rosenfels, who attempted the "John Elway Helicopter" against the Indianapolis Colts.

642. Kansas City Chiefs quarterback Patrick Mahomes.

643. Tampa Bay Buccaneers quarterback Tom Brady.

644. The New York Giants' Odell Beckham Jr.

645. Dallas Cowboys defensive tackle Leon Lett, who was playing against the Miami Dolphins on Thanksgiving.

646. Minnesota Vikings defensive end Jim Marshall.

647. Cleveland Browns linebacker Dwayne Rudd.

648. Minnesota Vikings kicker Gary Anderson.

649. Washington Commanders' Joe Gibbs.

650. New Orleans Saints quarterback Aaron Brooks.

651. Oakland Raiders quarterback JaMarcus Russell.

652. True.

653. Buffalo Bills running back Thurman Thomas.

654. Detroit Lions linebacker Stephen Tulloch.

655. Washington Commanders quarterback Gus Frerotte.

656. Jim Marshall.

WHO SAID IT?: COMMENTATOR EDITION

657. Joe Buck.

658. Kevin Harlan.

659. Gus Johnson.

660. Booger McFarland.

661. Kevin Harlan.

662. John Madden.

663. Brady Quinn.

664. Scott Zolak.

665. Jim Nantz.

666. Ronde Barber.

CHAPTER 7
HALL OF FAME

PLAYERS

667. Quarterbacks Jim Kelly and Steve Young, defensive end Reggie White, and offensive lineman Gary Zimmerman all began their pro football careers in the USFL between 1983 and 1985.

668. Offensive lineman, Anthony Muñoz is the only Hall of Famer to play all of his professional games for the Bengals.

669. Playing for University of Southern California, Marcus Allen was the first running back for the Trojans to surpass 2,000 yards in a season, winning both the Heisman Trophy and a national championship. As a member of the Los Angeles Raiders, Allen won a regular season MVP, was a two-time Super Bowl winner, and was the Super Bowl XVIII (18) MVP.

670. Ray Guy is the only punter in the Hall of Fame and is joined by placekicker Morten Andersen and Jan Stenerud.

671. Jim Plunkett won the 1970 Heisman Trophy, and is the only winner ever from Stanford University. Plunkett was the first overall pick in the 1971 NFL Draft and won two Super Bowls with the Oakland/Los Angeles Raiders.

672. Cornerback Charles Woodson joined running back Paul Hornung (Notre Dame/Green Bay Packers), quarterback Roger Staubach (Navy/Dallas Cowboys), running back Tony Dorsett (Pittsburgh/Dallas Cowboys), and running back Marcus Allen (Southern California/LA Raiders) as the fifth player to earn a Heisman and Super Bowl win during their Hall of Fame career.

673. Wide receiver Lynn Swann of the Pittsburgh Steelers was a Hall of Fame finalist 14 times before finally being selected in 2001, 19 years after his retirement in 1982.

674. Navy's Roger Staubach.

675. Fullback Jim Taylor was part of the Green Bay Packers' Super Bowl I (1) winning team and was part of the Hall of Fame Class of 1976.

676. Earl Campbell won the 1977 Heisman Trophy while at the University of Texas and was part of the Hall of Fame Class of 1991 after playing in the NFL from 1978 to 1985.

677. Dan Fouts (Los Angeles Chargers), Jim Kelly (Buffalo Bills), and Dan Marino (Miami Dolphins) are the only three quarterbacks since 1967 who played their entire career and reached the Hall of Fame without a Super Bowl ring.

678. Drew Pearson of the Dallas Cowboys played from 1973 to 1983 and entered the Hall of Fame with 7,822 yards, the fewest yards among wide receivers who played in the Super Bowl era.

679. Quarterback Steve Young, whose great-grandfather Brigham Young founded the Utah university that bears the same name.

680. B. Floyd Little (Denver Broncos, 1967 to 1975) had 6,323 rushing yards during his career, the fewest among any running back in the Hall of Fame.

681. D. Dallas Cowboys' quarterback Roger Staubach, with 22,700 yards, has the fewest passing yards of any Super Bowl–era quarterback in the Hall of Fame.

682. Defensive tackle John Randle joined the Minnesota Vikings in 1990 as an undrafted free agent and played 14 seasons, recording at least one sack in each of them, before being enshrined in the Hall of Fame in 2010.

683. Warren Moon was an undrafted quarterback coming out of the University of Washington, forcing him to play with the Edmonton Eskimos of the Canadian Football League from 1978 to 1983.

He then joined the Houston Oilers in 1984, playing for them until 1993. Moon retired with 49,325 NFL passing yards and 291 touchdowns, enough to earn himself a gold jacket.

684. The New Orleans Saints' Morten Andersen and Kansas City Chiefs' Jan Stenerud.

685. Florida State, Ohio State, and Southern California have combined to send zero quarterbacks to the Pro Football Hall of Fame.

686. Los Angeles Rams defensive tackle Merlin Olsen.

687. Quarterback Kurt Warner, who played for the St. Louis Rams (NFL) and the Iowa Barnstormers (AFL).

688. Bob Griese, whose son Brian Griese was the backup to John Elway on the Denver Broncos Super Bowl–winning team.

689. Oakland Raiders offensive lineman Gene Upshaw, who was inducted into the Hall of Fame in the summer of 1987. During the 1987 season, Upshaw, who was then the head of the NFL Players Association, called for a midseason strike that wiped out one week of the season and saw franchises throw together "scab" teams for three additional weeks until the strike was settled.

690. Running back Jim Thorpe played 289 Major League Baseball games (New York Giants) from 1913 to 1919, before playing 52 NFL games from 1920 to 1928. Cornerback Deion Sanders played 641 MLB games (New York Yankees, Atlanta Braves, Cincinnati Reds, and San Francisco Giants) from 1989 to 2001, while also playing 188 NFL games (Atlanta Falcons, Dallas Cowboys, San Francisco 49ers, the Washington Commanders, and Baltimore Ravens) from 1989 to 2005, enough to reach the Pro Football Hall of Fame.

691. Cal Hubbard, who played nine NFL seasons (1927 to 1936) as a New York Giants and Green Bay Packers defensive lineman, earning enshrinement in the Pro Football Hall of Fame in 1963. In 1976, Hubbard was inducted into the National Baseball Hall of Fame after working as a minor league and major league umpire from 1928 to 1969.

692. New Orleans Saints kicker Morten Andersen, who was born in Denmark.

693. Pittsburgh Steelers quarterback Terry Bradshaw.

694. Green Bay Packers quarterback Brett Favre.

695. St. Louis Rams and Arizona Cardinals quarterback Kurt Warner.

696. New York Jets quarterback Joe Namath.

697. Tony Boselli.

698. Billy Shaw.

699. Joe Klecko.

COACHES

700. Al Davis was the head coach of the Oakland Raiders from 1963 to 1965, before becoming the AFL commissioner in 1966. Davis also owned the Raiders from 1966 until his death in 2011.

701. Bud Grant (Minnesota Vikings), Don Shula (Baltimore Colts/ Miami Dolphins), and Marv Levy (Buffalo Bills) are all in the Hall of Fame despite suffering four Super Bowl losses. Shula won two of his six career Super Bowl appearances as a head coach while Grant and Levy both went 0–4.

702. Paul Brown (Cleveland Browns and Cincinnati Bengals), Weeb Ewbank (Baltimore Colts and New York Jets), Sid Gillman (Los Angeles Rams, Los Angeles/San Diego Chargers and Houston Oilers), and Hank Stram (Dallas Texans, Kansas City Chiefs, and New Orleans Saints) all coached AFL and NFL teams during their Hall of Fame careers.

703. Super Bowl I (1) and II (2) winner Vince Lombardi was part of the Hall of Fame Class of 1971.

704. False. Only Mike Holmgren left the Walsh-led 49ers and won a title with another franchise, leading the Green Bay Packers to their Super Bowl XXXI (31) win over the New England Patriots.

705. Marty Schottenheimer, who coached the Cleveland Browns (1984 to 1988), Kansas City Chiefs (1989 to 1998), Washington Commanders (2001), and San Diego Chargers (2002 to 2006), earning a 200–126–1 career record (61.3 win percentage).

706. Bill Parcells coached the New York Giants (1983 to 1990), New England Patriots (1993 to 1996), New York Jets (1997 to 1999), and the Dallas Cowboys (2003 to 2006) during his Hall of Fame career.

707. D, A, C, E, B. Madden has 103 wins, Flores has 97, Lombardi has 96, Walsh has 92, and Johnson has 80.

708. Tom Coughlin and Mike Shanahan. Coughlin led the New York Giants to two Super Bowl victories and has a 170–150 overall record. Shanahan won back-to-back Super Bowls with the Denver Broncos and has a 170–138 career record. Coughlin and Shanahan are tied for the most wins for a Super Bowl–winning head coach not in the Hall of Fame.

709. Earl "Curly" Lambeau helped found the Green Bay Packers in 1919, played halfback for the team for 11 years, and was their head coach from 1919 to 1949. The Packers play at Lambeau Field.

710. Dick LeBeau, who was only a head coach for parts of three seasons with the Cincinnati Bengals (2000 to 2002), but put together a Hall of Fame career as a cornerback with the Detroit Lions. LeBeau averaged an interception every three games and had at least three interceptions every season from 1960 to 1971. LeBeau went on to be an outstanding defensive coordinator and was part of two Super Bowl–winning teams with the Pittsburgh Steelers (2005 and 2008).

711. John Madden coached the Oakland Raiders from 1969 to 1978, winning Super Bowl XI (11).

712. Marty Schottenheimer employed Bruce Arians, Bill Cowher, Tony Dungy, and Mike McCarthy during his head coaching career; Cowher and Dungy are members of the Hall of Fame.

713. Super Bowl XX (20) pitted Hall of Famer Raymond Berry (1973) and the New England Patriots against the Chicago Bears, led by Mike Ditka, who was enshrined into the Hall of Fame in 1988.

714. Joe Gibbs retired from the Washington Commanders after the 1992 season and was inducted into the Hall of Fame in 1996. Gibbs returned to the team as its head coach from 2004 to 2007.

715. George Allen. Allen was the head coach of the Los Angeles Rams for five seasons (1966 to 1970) before coaching the Washington Commanders for seven seasons (1971 1977) and amassed a 116–47–5 regular season record (118–54–5 overall). Allen only coached in one Super Bowl, losing to the Miami Dolphins 14–7 during their 17–0 season of 1972.

716. Super Bowl V (5), when the Baltimore Colts defeated the Dallas Cowboys on January 17, 1971. It was the first Super Bowl played after the death of Vince Lombardi on September 3, 1970, and the NFL renamed the trophy in his honor, as it has been named from that point forward.

717. Tom Flores and the Oakland Raiders won Super Bowl XV (15) over the Philadelphia Eagles (27–17) as one of two AFC Wild Card teams, winning one game at home over the Houston Oilers and road games over the Cleveland Browns and San Diego Chargers. The 1980 season was the third in the NFL to use a three division/two Wild Card playoff format.

718. John Madden had an extreme fear of flying.

719. Purdue University. The Kansas City Chiefs won Super Bowl IV (4), led by their head coach Hank Stram and their Super Bowl MVP quarterback Len Dawson.

720. Jimmy Johnson won the 1987 national championship with the University of Miami Hurricanes. Johnson then joined the Dallas Cowboys in 1989, where he won two Super Bowls, becoming the first to win championships on both the college and pro levels.

721. Paul Brown and Bill Cowher. Brown coached the Cleveland Browns for eight seasons, reaching the playoffs in the first six seasons. Cowher led the Pittsburgh Steelers to the postseason during his first six seasons with the team.

722. Paul Brown.

723. Fritz Pollard played and was a head coach for four teams in the early days of the NFL. He was inducted into the Hall of Fame as the first Black head coach.

724. Sid Gillman, who was inducted into the Pro Football Hall of Fame as a coach in 1983, then inducted into the College Football Hall of Fame as a coach in 1989.

OWNERS & EXECUTIVES

725. The AFC championship trophy is named for Lamar Hunt, a founder of the AFL and the founder and owner of the Kansas City Chiefs.

726. The NFC championship trophy is named for George Halas, a founder of the NFL and the longtime coach and owner of the Chicago Bears.

727. Dan Reeves, who moved the Rams from Cleveland to Los Angeles in 1946.

728. Art Rooney and his son Dan Rooney ran the Pittsburgh Steelers from 1933 until 2017. Both are enshrined in the Hall of Fame; their son/grandson Art Rooney II is the current owner of the franchise.

729. Ralph Wilson Jr., whose Buffalo Bills made Super Bowl XXV (25), XXVI (26), XXVII (27), and XXVIII (28).

730. Bill Polian was the general manager for three of the Buffalo Bills' four AFC championship teams. Polian was also the general manager of the Indianapolis Colts and watched Peyton Manning win Super Bowl XLI (41). Two years later, the Colts were 14–0 and had clinched home field advantage in the AFC, so the team rested their players for the last two games of the season. The Colts reached the Super Bowl in 2010 (XLIV (44)), but lost to the New Orleans Saints 31–17.

731. Ed and Steve Sabol created NFL Films, which changed how football fans enjoyed highlights each week when they added music, voiceovers, and cinematographic elements. Both are in the Hall of Fame.

732. Edward DeBartolo Jr. saw the San Francisco 49ers win five Super Bowls in a 14-year span, the best stretch in NFL history. DeBartolo was then embroiled in legal issues that included extortion, failing to report a felony, and sexual assault, which saw him plead guilty in one case, settle another out of court, and eventually give up control of the team in 2000. He was pardoned by President Trump in 2020.

733. Bobby Beathard is credited with engineering seven conference championship teams and four Super Bowl winners, but Beathard's greatest feat might be the Super Bowl XVII (17) Washington Commanders winning roster, which included 27 free agents.

734. Ron Wolf drafted 10 players who would reach the Hall of Fame for the Raiders franchise and, while working for the Green Bay Packers in 1991, traded a first-round draft pick to the Atlanta Falcons for quarterback Brett Favre.

735. Green Bay Packers general manager Earl "Curly" Lambeau and head coach Vince Lombardi ended their careers with the Washington Commanders.

736. Just two days after the assassination of President John F. Kennedy, NFL commissioner Pete Rozelle decided to play the full schedule of games on November 24, 1963, something the rival AFL did not do. Rozelle would call it the biggest mistake of his career.

737. George Young. With Wellington Mara fighting with his nephew Tim over the longtime struggling New York Giants, commissioner Pete Rozelle strongly urged the team to hire Young as their general manager. Young hired Bill Parcells, drafted Phil Simms, and went on to win two Super Bowls.

738. Right after leaving the Dallas Cowboys, Tex Schramm was the president of the World League of American Football, which played two seasons in Europe.

739. David Baker, who was the President of the Pro Football Hall of Fame. Just as NFL Commissioner Roger Goodell welcomes newly drafted players into the NFL, Baker welcomes those voted into the Hall of Fame with a hug when informing them of their selection. Jim Porter took over in 2021.

WHO SAID IT?

740. Pittsburgh Steelers running back Jerome Bettis uttered those words in 2015.

741. "Look up, get up, and don't ever give up" was the advice given by Dallas Cowboys wide receiver Michael Irvin in 2007.

742. Pittsburgh Steelers quarterback Terry Bradshaw longed to take one more snap from his longtime center Mike Webster when going into the Hall of Fame in 1989. When Webster went into the Hall of Fame in 1997, the two exchanged one more snap to fulfill Bradshaw's wish.

743. Green Bay Packers quarterback Brett Favre, making light of his NFL-record 336 interceptions.

744. Minnesota Vikings and New England Patriots wide receiver Randy Moss.

745. Oakland Raiders defensive end Howie Long.

746. Pittsburgh Steelers linebacker Jack Lambert.

747. San Francisco 49ers wide receiver Jerry Rice, who was inducted into the Hall of Fame in 2010.

748. Minnesota Vikings wide receiver Cris Carter, who was inducted into the Hall of Fame in 2013.

749. Indianapolis Colts quarterback Peyton Manning, who was inducted into the Hall of Fame in 2021.

750. St. Louis Rams quarterback Kurt Warner said this during his enshrinement in 2017.

ACKNOWLEDGMENTS

I must thank Rafael Thomas for helping me craft this book; his expertise in writing and sports knowledge is invaluable. Also, I would like to thank Rebecca Markley, who helped edit this book. Without her leadership, guidance, and amazing editing, this book truly would not have been possible. Last, I would like to thank everyone on the Callisto Media team that played any role in crafting this book.

ABOUT THE AUTHOR

Jerrett Holloway is the founder of and a contributing writer for TooAthletic.com. Jerrett grew up in the Philadelphia area and remains a fan of the Philadelphia Eagles. However, his favorite athlete is Tom Brady.